A Formula for
Financial Health

4 PRINCIPLES
Gratitude • Contentment • Trust • Humility

+ 4 PRACTICES
Debt-Free Living • Saving • Budgeting • Giving

REAL PROFIT

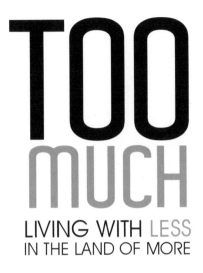

TOO MUCH

LIVING WITH LESS
IN THE LAND OF MORE

ISBN 978-0-692-54084-8

Cover Design by Gary Gogis – www.gogisdesign.com

Layout Design by Jake Stamper & Dustin Brenton – www.eclipsethem.com

Printing Services provided by Moeller Printing – www.moellerprinting.com

Dedicated

To my six grandchildren

Benaiah, Justin, Everly, Keturah, Nora and Abishai

who, I pray, will live out these biblical principles and practices,

bringing honor to God.

Acknowledgements

My sincere and heartfelt thanks to:

My wife, Leah, for her constant encouragement;

The Elders and staff of The Creek for their invaluable teamwork;

The people of The Creek for their unfailing support; and to

Gary Gogis, Jake Stamper, Dustin Brenton,

Jim Boling, Chuck Moeller, Karin Scheib, and Jason Yeatts

for their instrumental help in producing ***Too Much.***

FOREWORD

There are myriads of books on money, stewardship and related subjects. A simple Internet search reveals literally hundreds of choices. Some are interesting and helpful. Others are full of predictable platitudes in new packaging. Several seem like a forced effort to invent new abstract insights that aren't realistic or practical. Unfortunately, most will eventually gather dust and give a new definition to the term "shelf life".

By contrast, in *Too Much: Living with Less in the Land of More*, Gary Johnson has once again done what he does best. He has marshaled his considerable intellect, creativity, and experience to offer us a simple yet profound equation that provides tangible direction and strategy in the realm of personal finance. To those who know Gary this comes as no surprise. Gary simply does for his readers what he has done so well for thousands of people in his decades of ministry. He combines principles with practice to create a user-friendly resource that leads to tremendous spiritual and financial freedom.

This work is simply an overflow of the stewardship of life that Gary models so effectively. His energy, influence, giftedness, and passion all converge in this volume to provide principles and practices, which when internalized and implemented, will produce great benefits. Especially helpful are the "skin in the game" sections that will allow readers to immediately begin processing and practicing instead of waiting until the end of the book.

Many years ago, I listened as the president of my alma mater reminded students that one of the subjects Jesus spoke most often about was wealth. He suggested that nearly half the parables dealt with wealth, along with three of the Ten Commandments and nearly one out of every six verses in the gospels. He also claimed that the New Testament speaks sixteen times as much about money as it does about baptism and over thirty times as much about wealth as it speaks about the Lord's Supper. Admittedly, I never took the time to check the precise accuracy of his count and validate the exactness of his claims, but even if he was only close in his calculations—his arguments for the magnitude of this subject are unassailable. To state it in financial vernacular: we simply cannot afford to miss the "great gain" that comes from a Godly application of these pillar spiritual and financial realities.

So as you begin reading, perhaps it would be appropriate to start with this mindset. Imagine the exponential kingdom impact that will occur when we, as individual believers, begin to profit from the timeless wisdom of the God who created it all, owns it all, and distributes it all to those He entrusts with the management of His resources. It is my prayer that the following pages bring you genuine "profit" as you align yourself with the principles and practices herein.

Jeff Faull, Senior Minister

Mt. Gilead Church
Mooresville, Indiana

Table of Contents

Preface

Can't sleep? Tossing and turning through the night? If so, you may be among Americans who are losing sleep over money. A survey of one thousand adults by CreditCards.com revealed that sixty-two percent of those polled are unable to sleep because of money related issues in their lives. Six out of ten people. More than half. But there's good news! We don't have to lose sleep or stress out over money. We don't have to live with financial chaos. We can be free from the financial bondage of debt.

All across America, people have bought into the myth that more is never enough. When we pursue that lifestyle, we experience a number of unnecessary problems: stress in our marriages, arguments in our families, anxiety-related illnesses, tensions at work, and more. These are all symptoms of the *real* problem, and the *real* problem we face is living beyond our means. How do we learn to live with less in this land of more? Will we ever admit we have too much?

This book is structured on an equation: principles + practices = *real* profits. When we live by four key biblical principles, and then consistently pursue four simple financial practices, we will turn a *real* profit. The word profit means "a valuable return." Some books on personal finance emphasize actual financial profits. This book emphasizes *real* profits (i.e., valuable returns) that aren't always measured in dollars. When we learn to live with less, our marriages can be healed. We have time to enjoy with our families and friends—and even with our God. Valuable returns include having minimal or no debt, ample cash reserves, a commitment to tithing, to God-honoring generosity—and even restful sleep!

To implement this winning equation, we must live by four biblical principles: gratitude, contentment, trust, and humility while living out four simple practices: debt-free living, giving, budgeting, and saving. When we live by these principles and practices, they will produce *real* profit, the kind that is both enjoyable and God-honoring.

4 PRINCIPLES
Gratitude • Contentment • Trust • Humility

+ 4 PRACTICES
Debt-Free Living • Saving • Budgeting • Giving

REAL PROFIT

Keep in mind that learning to live with less in the land of more is a journey. We will not instantly experience the *real* profits of healed finances, relationships, and more. It takes time to dig ourselves into a financial pit, and it takes time to climb up and out. Increasing numbers of Americans are joining this journey. People are down-sizing. Instead of living in large, sprawling homes that consume time and resources to purchase and maintain, people are buying smaller homes—even tiny houses of 500 square feet or less are becoming popular.

As you read through this book, take time to pause and think about the principles and practices being explained. Take time to answer the reflection questions that appear throughout the chapters. If you are reading this with your spouse, with your family, or with a circle of friends in your small group, pause and discuss the questions with one another. Use this material to reach deeper places of life application.

The reflection questions will be marked by the phrase "SKIN IN THE GAME." Though we do not know the exact origin of this phrase, one legend indicates that when the internationally-known investor Warren Buffet began his now iconic career, he urged his original investors to generously ante up. At the same time, Buffet realized that he needed to invest some of his own money in the venture, too. Buffet had to have "SKIN IN THE GAME" if he was to sell others on this investment. This phrase implies more than money. Having SKIN IN THE GAME declares that we are courageously taking a risk by actually getting involved. For our finances to improve, we must personally and intentionally take action. We must boldly take a risk and live differently than we have in the past. Only then will we conquer the myth of more.

Why do I think I can write a book about personal finances? I am not a certified financial planner. I do not work in the financial industry. I am not a multi-millionaire. Because my wife Leah and I have learned to live with less and like it more, we have been completely debt free for a number of years. Our sons graduated from a private college without any student debt and we were able to pay cash for their educations. We live by the principles and practices mentioned in this book after we found them in another book: the Bible. Having served as a pastor for the last thirty-five years, I have learned a great deal about Scripture and its application to life. The Word has led our family to experience financial health in God-honoring ways. From time to time in this book, I relate bits and pieces of our life story to help illustrate a point being made.

Trust me, you do not have to lose sleep over money. Together, we can courageously admit that we have too much, even more than we can afford. We can live with less in the land of more – and even *like* it.

Chapter 1
The *Real* Problem

*"Thone who want to get rich fall into temptation
and a trap and into many foolish and harmful desires
that plunge people into ruin and destruction. For the love of money
is a root of all kinds of evil. Some people eager for money have wandered
from the faith and pierced themselves with many griefs."*
1 Timothy 6:9-10

"Houston, we have a problem." Those words are more than a well-known line from a movie. Those of us who are older remember when we first heard those words. Just two days into its mission to the moon in 1970, an oxygen supply tank exploded aboard Apollo 13. Captain James Lovell notified Mission Control that his crew had a life-threatening problem. News of the tragedy in space traveled quickly across America and around the world. If the three men aboard Apollo 13 were to survive, immediate and drastic action had to be taken by the crew and NASA's Mission Control in Houston. Everyone had to work together, and that they did. The three men returned safely to earth.

We have a problem, and it is so serious it will require all of us to work together for a solution. News of this problem has traveled across the United States and around the world. It is not related to an exploding oxygen supply tank. The problem we face is caused by exploding desires—especially the desire for more.

When I was growing up, stories of a particular person captured my attention. He was reclusive, and news of him was rare. When stories of this larger-than-life man made the newspaper, people were intrigued by the life that he lived. The guy wanted more in life. He wanted more money, and he became one of the first Americans to amass a multi-billion-dollar estate. He wanted fame, so he broke into the Hollywood scene and became a film-maker. He wanted more thrills, so he designed, built, and flew some of the fastest aircraft in the world. All he ever wanted was *more*. Yet, when his life came to an end, his body was emaciated and needle-scarred from his heavy drug use. His teeth had rotted. His fingernails were inches long and grotesquely shaped. The late Howard Hughes was a man who bought into the myth of more. For Hughes, more was never enough.

A MICRO-PROBLEM

As individuals, far too many of us struggle with the same problem that plagued Howard Hughes. More is never enough. Though the word "micro" means extremely small, this is not a small problem. It is a micro-problem in that it impacts us individually. Since the beginning of time, people run the risk of buying into this myth. Wanting more is deeply rooted within us.

Centuries ago, Jesus talked with a man whom we call "the rich, young ruler" (see Mark 10:17-23). Jesus invited the ruler to follow Him, but the young man declined the invitation: "He went away sad because he had great wealth" (verse 22). Jesus warned against buying into the myth of more: "Be on your guard against all kinds of greed; life does not consist in an abundance of possessions" (Luke 12:15); and following this warning, Jesus taught a parable about a rich man who wanted to build bigger and better barns for the storing of his grain and goods.

At the end of that parable, Jesus called the man a fool because his focus was on himself (verses 16-21).

The *real* problem is our inability to admit that we want and have too much. Whether single or married, rich or poor, young or old, when is more ever enough? At what point do we make enough money? How big do our homes or apartments need to be to satisfy us? How many pairs of jeans or shoes are enough? Is an extra freezer or pantry full of food enough? What about the books or tools we buy, the trips we take, and the cars we drive? When is enough really enough?

If we lived in a developing nation, we would not be talking about this right now. Poverty is dominant in many countries around the world. More than two billion people live on less than $2 a day. When we compare ourselves with people living in abject poverty, we are rich. When we compare ourselves to the Warren Buffets and Bill Gates of the world, we are poor. To get an idea of where we live on the income spectrum of people around the world, just go to www.globalrichlist.com, which quickly calculates where we rank globally when it comes to the amount of money we earn annually.

America is the land of plenty where there are endless opportunities of having more. Today, younger Americans want immediately what their parents worked a lifetime to accumulate. Older Americans, likewise, want their children to begin their young adult years with a standard of living similar to theirs. Those desires are rooted in the myth of more, and it is the *real* problem facing us as individuals—and as a nation.

SKIN IN THE GAME

▲ When we are ill, we often see a physician who does an exam and reaches a diagnosis. We should do the same with our finances. How healthy are you financially? What symptoms do you see? Are payments late? Is debt difficult to manage? How much discretionary spending can you safely afford? What is your diagnosis?

▲ Just as a physician identifies the cause of an illness, reflect on the cause of your financial illness. Do you buy into the myth of more? Have you determined when enough is actually enough?

A MACRO-PROBLEM

Buying into the myth of more is not only the *real* problem that we face on a personal (micro) scale, but it is easy to spot on a looming (macro) scale. Governments at all levels are susceptible of amassing debt because of always wanting more. This reality is true across the United States and around the world. Before long, the macro reinforces the micro. When we see entire governments head over heels in debt to finance the purchase of more, we come to think that such behavior is normal, and even acceptable. The old adage becomes real to us: since everybody is doing it, it must be right. Yet, living this way could not be more wrong. The *real* problem is a big problem on the macro-scale.

Do you remember the bail outs? During the Great Recession of 2008, one corporate giant after another needed the government to bail them out of a financial pit. Congress voted to bail out Freddie Mac and Fannie Mae to the tune of roughly $200 billion. Big banks received north of a combined $800 billion. Bear Stearns was given a financial leg-up of $29 billion and the insurance giant AIG was first rescued with $85 billion, and later requested an additional $37 billion. As the federal government provided loan bail outs in excess of $1 trillion to businesses, our own national financial nightmare grew worse. In 2008, our government was running a federal deficit in excess of $400 billion and Congress was debating whether to increase our national debt ceiling to over $11 trillion.

How did we get ourselves into such a mess? Moreover, how could global corporations and internationally powerful banks be bankrupt? The answer was in the news. An article on the front page of the *Indianapolis Star* stated, "America's brewing fiscal collapse has a common cause: a bankruptcy of values when it comes to money."[1] Talk about hitting the nail on the head! During the Great Recession of 2008, America put on display its bankruptcy of values when it came to money and the things money can buy. From corporate giants on Wall Street to individuals living on Main Street, a familiar cry was heard, "Bail me out!" Yet, America's bankruptcy of values with money did not end with the Great Recession. We still struggle when it comes to money.

The United States Treasury continues to operate on borrowed funds. As a nation, we are living beyond our means and have done so for years. Reports on www.treasury.gov show that since 1960, Congress has approved the increase of our national debt ceiling seventy-eight times! Currently, our national debt is in excess of $18 trillion, and if we fail to increase the debt ceiling, our government would default on its expenses and obligations. Social security payments would cease. Medicare benefits would come to an end. Military and government salaries would go unpaid, and tax refunds would not be processed. Think with me. If we added up all of the income made by Americans this year and used it to pay down our national debt, there would *still* be a substantial balance owed by our federal government! For a sobering reality of the macro-dimension of our national debt, just visit www.usdebtclock.org. Remember, the *real* problem behind our debt – whether personal or national – is our desire for more.

Like our federal government, a number of state and municipal govern-ments are crushed with debt because of living beyond their means. For example, during the Great Recession, the state of California was forced to issue IOUs to residents in lieu of checks. Why? California state government had run out of money, and both its debt and deficit were in the billions of dollars. California is not alone. Texas, New Jersey, and Illinois rank high in excessive debt. If we were to add up all of the debt owed by all fifty states, the number is in the trillions of dollars. Moreover, hundreds of cities across America have filed Chapter 9 bankruptcy, with the largest being Detroit in 2013. Detroit's debt exceeded an estimated $18-20 billion, making the city unable to meet its obligations. In recent decades, hundreds of cities have become financially insolvent. Why? More is never enough.

The myth of more has extended beyond our nation's borders. Countries around the world are awash in red ink. One nation often in the news is Greece, a nation that has been bailed out of its financial pit no less than three times by coun-tries of the European Union. Why? Greece's government has practiced unre-strained spending for years with guaranteed pensions starting at age sixty, provid-ing cradle-to-grave healthcare, and giving out nearly unlimited education benefits.[2]

Greece's national debt is actually larger than its national economy. Puerto Rico is facing a similar dilemma. Its government officials failed to make required bond payments, and now the island nation is in default on a $72 billion national debt. Puerto Rico is in a deep recession with little or no cash to keep the government operating.[3] If countries do not come to grips with uncontrolled spending, their futures will look like that of Greece and Puerto Rico—and that includes our country's future, as well.

Regretfully, the list of countries, states, and municipalities that are crushed by the weight of debt is seemingly endless. Remember, the *real* problem that fuels debt is buying into the myth that more is never enough, and governments of all shapes and sizes are having to deal with this macro-problem.

Though the Apollo 13 moon mission had a fairy-tale happy ending, NASA experienced a great tragedy just a few years later. After landing on the moon, NASA moved into the space shuttle era. On January 28, 1986, the space shuttle *Challenger* was scheduled to launch, but it was delayed because of unseasonably cold weather. Allan McDonald, an engineer from Morton-Thiokol, the company that built the solid-rocket engines that would propel the *Challenger* high into space, was greatly concerned about the o-rings used in the engine joints. The engines had not been tested in temperatures below fifty-three degrees, so McDonald recommended that the launch be delayed once again. Yet, NASA officials overruled him. Just seventy-three seconds into the launch, the space shuttle *Challenger* exploded. The cause of explosion was later determined to be the failure of the o-rings to function in cold temperatures.

Why did NASA officials ignore the warning and give permission for *Challenger's* launch? McDonald said, "NASA (had become) too successful. They had gotten by for a quarter of a century and had never lost a single person going into space…And they had rescued the Apollo 13 halfway to the moon when part of the vehicle blew up. Seemed like it was an impossible task, but they did it. So how could this cold o-ring cause a problem when they had done so much over the past years to be successful? (All of this success) gives you a little bit of arrogance you shouldn't have…But they hadn't stumbled yet and they just pressed on."[4] It appears that pride really does go before a fall.

Will pride be our downfall? Whether on a macro or micro scale, will we admit to having a problem with money and with the things that money can buy? Will we realize that the *real* problem is wanting more? Can we get to the place in life where we say that we have too much, and we want to live with less in the land of more?

Friend, we have a problem, but it can be solved. Read on.

SKIN IN THE GAME

▲ We don't have to be on the edge of financial collapse to improve our financial health. Do you really want to learn to live with less in the land of more? If so, what is your plan?

▲ Will you go on this journey with someone – a spouse, a friend, a small group, etc.? Will you ask someone to help hold you accountable to putting into practice what you learn? If so, who is that person?

▲ Will you teach what you learn about money and its management to your children or grandchildren?

▲ Proverbs 16:3 reads: "Commit to the Lord whatever you do and your plans will succeed." Will you dedicate this journey to financial health to the glory of God, honoring Him with the results?

Chapter 2
The Principle of Gratitude

"Give thanks in all circumstances,
for this is God's will for you in Christ Jesus."
1 Thessalonians 5:18

Cereal. It's enough to make a grown man cry. Sasha Moravski did. I saw him weep when we turned the corner into the cereal aisle at the Kroger store. It took me a moment to realize what was happening. Sasha was a worship pastor from Ukraine, and he came to stay with us some years ago for an internship to learn about ministry in the local church. Ukraine became independent from the former Soviet Union in 1991, but it immediately faced great financial hardship. Ukrainians, including Sasha's family, found it difficult to buy even the most basic foods: bread, milk, eggs, sugar, meat of any kind, etc. When I stayed in Sasha's home a few years prior to his visit to America, I remember seeing one banana thinly sliced, arranged on a saucer and put on the table for the entire family to share. So, I wasn't surprised when he broke down and cried in the cereal aisle. He kept saying, "Americans have so much." Too much.

Come to think of it, we have so much that we become ungrateful. We take our bountiful lives for granted. We may be in bondage financially, yet we live in a free land. We may struggle living paycheck to paycheck, but I doubt that any of us go to bed hungry. We have beds in which to sleep, roofs over our heads, and clothes on our backs. We live in a land where technology abounds and educational opportunities are unlimited. We are blessed beyond measure in this land of plenty.

So, what's our problem? Simply put: we have too much; and when we have too much, we take too much for granted. Even now, you may be thinking that my comments are out of line. You may argue that I am wrong when I say that we have too much. How have I reached that conclusion? Don't look around and compare yourselves to the Bill Gates, Warren Buffets, or the Donald Trumps of the world. Don't look at the CEO of your company who makes tens of thousands—if not millions—more than the rest of us. Instead, look around at how the rest of the world lives. Many sources report that 2 billion people live on $2 or less a day. Imagine that. How can that be? Most people live in deep poverty, but not us. We have too much, which results in our taking too much for granted.

SKIN IN THE GAME

▲ Go to www.globalrichlist.com and enter your income. Notice your rank in world income. Surprised? How about shocked? Did you realize how wealthy you are?

▲ Identify different aspects of life: vocation, marriage, family, friendships, health, education, money, possessions, etc. Do you take anything for granted in these areas? If so, what?

GREED VERSUS GRATITUDE

Do you like to eat? I do, especially during the holidays. My wife is a great cook and I like walking into the house when the turkey and homemade bread are baking. An incredible smell hangs heavy in the air as Leah prepares a holiday feast. Some things never change. Jesus Himself experienced a holiday feast given in His honor. That meal is described in the Gospel of John, and if we look carefully, we can notice that something was hanging heavy in the air at that feast, too.

John 12:1-8

Six days before the Passover, Jesus arrived at Bethany, where Lazarus lived, whom Jesus had raised from the dead. Here a dinner was given in Jesus' honor. Martha served, while Lazarus was among those reclining at the table with Him. Then Mary took about a pint of pure nard, an expensive perfume; she poured it on Jesus' feet and wiped His feet with her hair. And the house was filled with the fragrance of the perfume. But one of the disciples, Judas Iscariot, who was later to betray him, objected, "Why wasn't this perfume sold and the money given to the poor? It was worth a year's wages." He did not say this because he cared about the poor but because he was a thief; as keeper of the money bag, he used to help himself to what was put into it. "Leave her alone," Jesus replied. "It was intended that she should save this perfume for the day of My burial. You will always have the poor among you, but you will not always have Me."

This was an incredible holiday gathering. Formal meals were special occasions. Men would recline on couches called tricliniums that were arranged around a central table covered with food. With their hands, they would reach forward towards the food, while their feet extended off the end of the couch. Imagine Jesus looking over His shoulder seeing Mary pouring perfume on His feet, then wiping His feet with her hair. Imagine hearing the gasps of the other dinner guests at the sight of this brazen act! Never would a Jewish woman let her hair down in public. Moreover, the extravagant cost of the perfume crossed the mind of at least one person in the room, if not others. It was pure nard, not a synthetic or generic nard. It was an herb grown so far away in the high pastures of the Himalayas of Tibet and India that harvesting and transporting the perfume made it highly valued. Yet, Mary did the unthinkable. She broke the jar open and poured out its entire contents on the feet of Jesus. Immediately, the smell of the nard hung heavy in the air—and so did something else.

Greed. The greed was so thick that it could be cut with a knife. You see, a thief was sitting at the dinner table. Judas Iscariot stole money from Jesus; and when he saw the perfume running onto the floor, it threw him into a rage because greed ruled him. For Judas, *more was never enough*. Judas complained loudly about the waste. The perfume could have been sold and the money given to the poor. This holiday meal happened in the village of Bethany, meaning "house of the poor." Hungry, poor people were everywhere in Bethany. Did Judas take for granted the privilege of being a disciple of Jesus and of being in His presence every day? Did he take for granted being a witness to the many miracles of Jesus or the honor of hearing Jesus preach and teach? I think so. Judas had so many privileges and blessings that he took them for granted. The result? Greed. More was never enough for him.

Something else hung heavy in the air that night. Cutting through the stench of greed was the aroma of gratitude. Look behind the scene to the custom of the day. When someone died, his or her corpse was anointed with spices and perfumes and then placed in a family tomb. When the tomb was later reopened for the burial of other relatives, the spices and perfumes would help soften the strong smell of decomposition. Instead of waiting until His death, Mary poured out her extravagant gift on the feet of Jesus, expressing her profound gratitude to

CHAPTER 2 · THE PRINCIPLE OF GRATITUDE

31

Him. Remember, this holiday meal was in the home of Mary's brother Lazarus, the one whom Jesus previously raised from the dead. Mary was grateful that Jesus brought her brother back to life and that someday Jesus would also raise her from the dead. Mary believed that Jesus was her Messiah and that He had come to bring her life everlasting. Pouring the expensive perfume over His feet, Mary did more than fill the air with the smell of pure nard. She filled the room with deep, heartfelt gratitude.

What hangs heavy in the air of our lives—greed or gratitude? Are we like Judas? Are we preoccupied with money and the things that money can buy? Jesus said that a person cannot serve both God and money (Matthew 6:24). This was obvious with Judas. He could not serve Christ and money. Greed ruled Judas until the end of his life when he sold out Jesus for thirty pieces of silver. We, too, can easily fall prey to greed. Even at birth we have this tendency. As babies, our cute, cuddly bodies are filled with "greedy-genes." Babies cry when they want something. They want to be fed, changed, or held—now! When toddlers learn to talk, one of their first words is, "Mine!" Toddlers scream, "Mine!" while grabbing toys away from other toddlers. If left unchecked, greedy-genes grow with us into adulthood. It is no surprise, then, that left to itself, the human heart hoards. We want more while taking for granted what we already have. Not until a person acknowledges his or her greedy nature can transformation happen.

Are we like Mary? Are we grateful for what God has done, is doing, and will do in our lives? Do we give thanks to God – repeatedly and sincerely? This is not simply saying some half-baked prayer, "God is great, God is good, let us thank Him for our food. Amen." The Apostle Paul said, "Give thanks in all circumstances, for this is God's will for you in Christ Jesus" (I Thessalonians 5:18). Paul was whipped, beaten, abused with stones, and left for dead. Paul was shipwrecked three times, spending a day and night in the open sea. He was threatened with theft by robbers and with murder by his own countrymen. He was often hungry and thirsty while being imprisoned for years (2 Corinthians 11:24-27). Yet, Paul said confidently, "Give thanks—in all circumstances." He repeatedly urged Christ-followers to be grateful.

Colossians 3:15-17

Let the peace of Christ rule in your hearts, since as members of one body you were called to peace. *And be thankful.* Let the message of Christ dwell among you richly as you teach and admonish one another with all wisdom through psalms, hymns, and songs from the Spirit, singing to God *with gratitude in your hearts.* And whatever you do, whether in word or deed, do it all in the name of the Lord Jesus, *giving thanks to God the Father through him.* (italics mine)

In this section of his letter to the Colossian Christians, Paul declares not once, but three times to give thanks to God. Like a mother teaching her children to say "thank you," Paul taught people again and again to express gratitude to God. Why? Developing a grateful heart indicates that we are growing more spiritually mature. Paul experienced this himself. Not only did he grow old in the faith, but he grew up in the faith. There is a difference, and it's a big one. Paul developed a heart of profound gratitude within him, and he understood that a mark of spiritual maturity is being a truly grateful person. The level of our gratitude is a reflection of how spiritually mature we are. If you and I want to be strong, mature Christians, we must work with God to become grateful Christians, men and women who are full of thanksgiving. Give thanks.

CHAPTER 2 · THE PRINCIPLE OF GRATITUDE

SKIN IN THE GAME

▲ Do you wish for more? Does an advertisement stir you to say, "I wish I had that"? Are you envious of those who have more than you? Be honest. Can you spot the spirit of greed growing in you? If so, how is greed showing itself in your life?

▲ Do you take for granted what you already have? Is gratitude missing from your life? When was the last time you sent a handwritten thank you note to someone? Who received it and why? How often do you pray prayers of thanksgiving? For what do you thank God? How heavy does gratitude hang in the air of your life?

What can we do to grow gratitude within us? If I were to ask you to look around and spot everything that is the color red, you could easily do that because you are specifically looking for a certain color. Likewise, if we deliberately look around us we can easily spot the many blessings of God in our lives. Psalm 27:13 states, "I remain confident of this: I will see the goodness of the Lord in the land of the living." Do we look for the goodness of the Lord or for what we want or wish we had? Are we blind to His goodness? If so, it is an indication we taking too much for granted in this land where we have too much.

Years ago, when our sons were very young, Leah and I started keeping "I Spy" journals based on Psalm 27:13. At the end of the day, we would sit and write in the journal how we spied "the goodness of the Lord in the land of the living." As a family, we wanted to intentionally focus on all of God's blessings around us each day, and this helped us grow more grateful. If we look for the color red in a room, we will be able spot it. The same is true for spotting the goodness of the Lord. If we deliberately go looking for it, we will find it. Every day, I can easily see the mercy, grace, kindness, and goodness of the Lord; and for this, I am overwhelmingly thankful. We cannot thank God too much. I have often thought, what would happen if we woke up today with only what we thanked God for yesterday? This is a sobering thought. We need God's help. Pray this prayer: *"Dear God, teach me to be grateful for what I have before time forces me to be grateful for what I had."*

THE WHO AND THE WHY BEHIND GRATITUDE

The primary reason why greed hangs heavy in the air of our lives is that we have forgotten God in this land of more. This phenomenon is not new. When the Israelites were about to enter into the Promised Land, Moses spoke of this same issue.

Deuteronomy 8:1-4

Be careful to follow every command I am giving you today, so that you may live and increase and may enter and possess the land that the Lord promised on oath to your forefathers. Remember how the Lord your God led you all the way in the desert these forty years, to humble you and to test you in order to know what was in your heart, whether or not you would keep His commands. He humbled you, causing you to hunger and then feeding you with manna, which neither you nor your fathers had known, to teach you that man does not live on bread alone but on every word that comes from the mouth of the Lord. Your clothes did not wear out and your feet did not swell during these forty years.

The act of remembering is important. It was back then and it still is today. Deuteronomy is a collection of final sermons that Moses preached to the millions of Israelites before they entered the Promised Land. In sermon after sermon, Moses told the people to remember God. No less than thirteen times, Moses urged the Israelites to impress upon their minds, and recall in conversation, God's supernatural provision while they lived for decades in the wilderness. God alone provided food for them in a land where they could not grow their own food. He alone provided water in a desert wasteland where there were no lakes or deep wells. God made their clothes to last for years. Moses commanded them to deliberately dwell on the fact that God was their Provider, the One who gave them all that they needed to live on from day-to-day. But, that was not Moses' only message in his final sermons. He gave them a warning before they moved into the Promised Land—the land of plenty.

Deuteronomy 8:10-14

When you have eaten and are satisfied, praise the Lord your God for the good land He has given you. Be careful that you do not forget the Lord your God, failing to observe His commands, His laws and His decrees that I am giving you this day. Otherwise, when you eat and are satisfied, when you build fine houses and settle down, and when your herds and flocks grow large and your silver and gold increase and all you have is multiplied, then your heart will become proud and you will forget the Lord your God, who brought you out of Egypt, out of the land of slavery.

That is exactly what happened. No sooner had they moved into the land of plenty that they forgot God, their Provider. While sitting at tables covered with food, while living in fine homes with roofs over their heads, while gold and silver accumulated in their investment accounts, the people of God forgot their God. They began to see themselves as the source of their bounty.

Deuteronomy 8:17-20

You may say to yourself, "My power and the strength of my hands have produced this wealth for me." But remember the Lord your God, for it is He who gives you the ability to produce wealth, and so confirms His covenant, which He swore to your ancestors, as it is today. If you ever forget the Lord your God and follow other gods and worship and bow down to them, I testify against you today that you will surely be destroyed. Like the nations the Lord destroyed before you, so you will be destroyed for not obeying the Lord your God.

Nothing has changed. Moses could stand in our churches and preach the same sermons to people who live and think in the same way. In our land of plenty, we have forgotten that our God is our Provider, that He alone is the source of all that we have. God gives us mental and physical abilities to produce income. He alone gives us the ability to build fine houses and to eat good food. We think it is by the work of our hands and by the sweat of our brows that we have produced all that we have. It is ours—at least in our thinking. But, King David reminds us: "The earth is the Lord's and everything in it; the world and all who live in it" (Psalm 24:1).

The truth is simply that everything we have comes from God and is owned by God, even our very lives. The Apostle Paul reminds us of this fact, "Do you not know that your bodies are temples of the Holy Spirit, who is in you, whom you have received from God? You are not your own, you were bought with a price. Therefore honor God with your bodies" (1 Corinthians 6:19-20). We're not the owners of anything. We're leasing everything—even our bodies! We're caretakers or stewards, managers of everything that belongs to God. As care-takers or stewards, we do not merely possess things; we properly use those things He has allowed us to possess.

The position of caretaker was created at the beginning of time, even before the first sin was committed. God made Adam the caretaker of the Garden of Eden (Genesis 2:8, 15). The description of the position has not changed. Think with me. If I borrow your condominium for vacation, I'm going to take care of it while using it and thoroughly clean it before I return the keys to you. The same must be true of our relationship to God. We must take care of all that He has entrusted to us because there will come a time when we "return the keys of our lives" to Him. He is the source of the provisions in our lives and we must take care of these provisions—not merely possessing them, but using properly what we possess.

The first essential part of our journey to financial freedom is a radical change in attitude. We must willingly acknowledge that God is the source of all that we have, and that He is sovereign over every part of our lives—from all of our money to all that money can buy. God gives us not only the ability to earn money, but also the opportunities to accumulate it, to spend it, and give it away.

SKIN IN THE GAME

▲ Let's close our eyes—and see everything we own. Now, let's open our eyes—and see everything God owns. How can we actually begin to think this way?

▲ In our minds, we must transfer the title to the car, the deed to the house, the contents of the investment portfolio, the balance in the checking and savings account – over to God. Talk about what that means. Pray a prayer of "transfer" to God— and be sincere.

THROUGH THE EYES OF A CHILD

The Johnsons are connoisseurs of M&Ms. No matter their size, shape, color, or content, we buy them and eat them. We keep a good supply on hand because our grandchildren have also grown to love M&Ms. God has revealed some insights to me through the world of M&Ms and my grandchildren.

If I take my grandchildren to the movies and I buy them each a bag of M&Ms, I will ask them for one or two from time to time through the movie (that is, if they last that long). When they deny me even one M&M, a truth is made known to me—and hopefully to them. I was the one who supplied them with M&Ms. They would not have those chocolate covered treats if it were not for Grandpa. Moreover, I wonder if they realize that I could "bury" them neck-deep in M&Ms. For that matter, I could go and get all the M&Ms I could ever want. Moreover, do they realize that just as I generously gave them M&Ms, I can take them away at any moment? All I want to do is experience a moment with my grandchildren—watching a movie together, eating one of our favorite treats, and from time to time hearing a tiny voice whisper in the dark theater, "Thank you, Grandpa!"

You and I are children of God. He has poured out blessings beyond measure to us, and He wants us to share with Him a portion of what He's lavished on us. Just as He has given us all our blessings, He can remove them because He alone is sovereign. He wants to hear us say each day a heartfelt, "Thank you, God!" He knows that gratitude is necessary for us to stay connected to His love, and it allows us not to forget Him like the Israelites did in the desert.

On December 15, 1967—just ten days before Christmas—the Silver Bridge collapsed into the Ohio River in Point Pleasant, West Virginia. Traffic was bumper-to-bumper on the bridge at five in the afternoon. People were leaving downtown Point Pleasant at the end of the work day, while others were driving downtown to do their Christmas shopping. Eyewitnesses reported that a sound like that of a sonic-boom erupted, anchor cables at the end of the bridge ripped from deep in the earth, and the bridge fell into the water below, claiming the lives of forty-six people. The U.S. Army Corps of Engineers determined that the tragedy was caused by the failure of a single metal eyebolt. When this one piece of metal gave way, it caused the massive collapse and loss of life. A simple piece of metal was missing.[5]

Is gratitude missing from your life? Do you take for granted all the blessings of God entrusted to you? If we take too much for granted, it is directly related from having too much in this land of more. If our gratitude to God (and others) is missing, we should not be surprised when our finances collapse around us. The collapse will not only impact us individually, but also the innocent lives of our family and loved ones. Pursue gratitude—the first principle in the equation that results in financial freedom. Give thanks.

SKIN IN THE GAME

▲ Develop an obsession for giving thanks to God. Pray through the alphabet giving thanks for something specific that begins with every letter. Name the top-ten things for which you are grateful. Wake up thanking God. Go to sleep thanking God. We cannot thank God too much.

▲ Do we get upset when people fail to thank us when we do something nice for them? Do we feel hurt when someone doesn't thank us when we give them a gift? Talk about how God must feel when we fail to thank Him.

Chapter 3
The Principle of Contentment

"Godliness with contentment is great gain."
1 Timothy 6:6

I received an inheritance from my dad. He died suddenly of a stroke at the age of seventy-six. His death caught me, and my two brothers, by surprise. But what I inherited from my dad surprised me more.

As the executor of my parents' estate, I knew every detail about their bank accounts and real estate deeds. There were no outstanding debts to pay nor stock portfolios to manage. When the house and cabin were sold and the savings account closed, my brothers and I received a modest inheritance. At least, most people would see it that way. From my vantage point, however, I inherited from my dad something worth far more than dollars and cents. He gave me an inheritance I have drawn on time and again over the years.

What did I inherit? Here's part of my story. My dad was married to my mom for fifty-two years on the day that she died. My dad retired from a job that he held from the time of his high school graduation. He even worked in the same department his entire life. My dad died in the same house where he lived since he was seven years old. In short, he had one wife, one job, and one address for his entire life. These are just three examples of the many ways in which my dad modeled for me an important principle: being content. My dad was truly content "with the wife of his youth" (Proverbs 5:18). He was also content where he lived. When the time came for him to care for his aging mother, he did not buy a new and bigger house; rather, he remodeled his home and added an apartment for her. My dad stayed at the same job his entire career, and even started a small construction-related business that he ran after getting out of work at the factory each afternoon. The need for more was not a part of my dad's thinking. He learned to be content, and he passed that principle down to me.

Contentment. It is the second of four key biblical principles leading to financial freedom. Remember, this book is structured on an equation: principles + practices = *real* profit. The word profit means "a valuable return," and when we live by four certain principles and implement four simple life-long practices, we will experience *real* financial freedom. Contentment plays a big part in the equation. As we dig into this principle, keep in mind that we are not born content. It is an attitude we learn. Some people have it and some people don't. It's easy to spot the "have nots" and the "haves" in Scripture.

THE HAVE NOTS

Solomon. Though he had everything a man could ever want, Solomon was a "have not" when it came to contentment. Near the end of his life, Solomon wrote the book of Ecclesiastes. He looked back over his life and reached one conclusion—everything was meaningless. "Meaningless! Meaningless! Everything is meaningless!" That sentence appears over and over again in Ecclesiastes. Why would Solomon reach such a conclusion? I believe it is because he had *too much*—too much of everything.

In the opening two chapters, Solomon wrote that he had great wisdom, more so than any of the previous rulers of Israel (Ecclesiastes 1:16). He explained how he tried cheering himself with wine, but that did not bring him fulfillment any more than the work of his hands (Ecclesiastes 2:3-4). Solomon amassed immeasurable wealth and he had a harem of women—seven hundred wives and three hundred concubines (Ecclesiastes 2:7-8, 1 Kings 11:3). Wisdom. Wine. Work. Wealth. Women. Solomon even admitted, "Whoever loves money never has money enough; whoever loves wealth is never satisfied with their income. This too is meaningless. As goods increase, so do those who consume them. And what benefit are they to the owners except to feast their eyes on them?" (Ecclesiastes 5:10-11) Simply put, Solomon had an insatiable thirst for more; and for him, more was never enough. Solomon did not learn to be content with what he had.

Another "have not" who stands out in Scripture is a guy who met up with Jesus. Who was he? We call him the rich, young ruler. His story is told in Matthew, Mark, and Luke (Mt 19:16f, Mark 10:17f, Luke 18:18f). Each account tells us about what he was like, which is how we get his nickname: the "rich, young ruler."

This man was wealthy, powerful, and young. Moreover, it appears that he was careful to obey the Old Testament Law. Yet, something weighed on his mind, so he ran to Jesus, fell on his knees, and asked, "Good Teacher, what must I do to inherit eternal life?" Jesus looked at him and loved him, and then said, "One thing you lack. Go, sell everything you have and give to the poor, and you will have treasure in heaven. Then come, follow Me." (Mark 10:17-22). This rocked the world of the rich, young ruler because he refused to follow Jesus. He didn't just have a lot of stuff. His stuff had him. Ultimately, this rich, young man did not have contentment.

How about just one more "have not?" Jesus spoke of him in Luke 12:13-21. I call him "the barn guy," and he had the starring role in a parable that Jesus told. In the story, there was a farmer ("the barn guy") who had a bumper harvest and nowhere to store it. So he reasoned that he should tear down his existing barns and build bigger ones. Then he would have plenty of space to store his grain and farm equipment.

Jesus didn't fault the barn guy because he had a great harvest or great wealth. There is nothing sinful about being successful or wealthy. Yet, this guy had two serious problems: 1) he never saw beyond his life, and 2) he never saw beyond this life. The barn guy was consumed with himself. No other parable has such an extensive use of the first person singular pronouns (i.e., "I," "me," and "my"). Jesus called the guy a fool! His life was demanded of him one night. He was held accountable for being greedy and for failing to be rich towards God. In other words, he was a dead man! Come to think of it, he was already a dead man. He was self-indulgent and self-centered. Although he had much, there was something he lacked. According to the world's standards, he appeared to be one of "the haves," but in reality, he was a "have not." He did not have contentment as a part of his life.

The "have nots" are still with us today, and we are those people. How content are we? Fortune and fame. Power and pleasure. We worship at the shrine of more. More money, more fame, more power, more pleasure—it's never enough. So, we work long hours to earn more money to afford more debt to buy and do more things all because we are not content with what we have.

SKIN IN THE GAME

▲ How can you avoid end-of-life regrets like those of Solomon?

▲ The rich, young ruler had a lot of stuff, but his stuff had him. We have a lot of stuff. In what ways and to what degree does your stuff have you?

▲ "I, me, my, mine." How often do you hear yourself using these first person singular pronouns in conversation? When conversing with others, do you find yourself needing to "one-up" others? If so, how and when will you stop that behavior?

THE HAVES

The Apostle Paul was one of the most prolific authors of the New Testament, and a number of his letters were written from behind prison bars. Paul was arrested many times for being a follower of Jesus Christ; while he was incarcerated, he wrote letters to many churches. His letter to the church at Philippi was one of them, and in it he wrote a lot about joy. Although short in length, this letter includes the word "joy"—or a form of it—no less than sixteen times. Remember Paul was writing from behind bars (Philippians 1:13)! One portion of the letter makes it clear that he had something that others did not. Check this out.

Philippians 4:10-16

I rejoice greatly in the Lord that at last you have renewed your concern for me. Indeed, you have been concerned, but you had no opportunity to show it. I am not saying this because I am in need, for I have learned to be content whatever the circumstances. I know what it is to be in need, and I know what it is to have plenty. I have learned the secret of being content in any and every situation, whether well fed or hungry, whether living in plenty or in want. I can do everything through him who gives me strength. Yet it was good of you to share in my troubles. Moreover, as you Philippians know, in the early days of your acquaintance with the gospel, when I set out from Macedonia, not one church shared with me in the matter of giving and receiving, except you only; for even when I was in Thessalonica, you sent me aid again and again when I was in need.

Paul was one of the "haves" in the Bible who had contentment in his life. He learned to be content, whether he had much or little. The word "content" means to be satisfied. Paul was satisfied with what he had, even though it was so little, particularly while behind bars. From the world's point of view, he was shackled. From God's perspective, he was a free man. He was free from the trappings of materialism. He did not struggle with the cancer of greed. Paul lived a simple life, free from the need to impress people with what he owned or what he did. Having learned to be content, Paul lived with less in a land of more.

Be sure to notice that Paul wasn't born content. He had to learn this attitude and behavior. Just as Paul learned how to walk, talk, read, and write, he also learned how to be content—how to be satisfied with whatever he had in life – whether having plenty or living in want. The phrase "learned the secret of being content" means to be initiated. It is a verb that is used only here in the New Testament Greek and it implies a mystery. Mysteriously, Paul experienced a rare initiation into this life of contentment–going without the creature comforts of life. He went through some pretty tough conditioning and was initiated into this new way of living that involved hunger, thirst, physical suffering, persecution, and more. But it also involved joy.

How can we possibly admit that we have *too much*? It has everything to do with learning to be content with what we already have and saying that enough is enough. No more! For that to happen in our lives, we must echo a statement of the Apostle Paul: "I can do all this through Him who gives me strength" (Philippians 4:13).

This verse is one of the most misused verses in the Bible. An individual will say, "I can lose ten pounds because I can do all things through Christ who gives me strength;" or "I can get that new job, because I can do everything through Christ who gives me strength." When we interpret the content of Scripture, we must first consider the context of Scripture. The context of this passage is about Paul learning to be content, and the possibility of the same happening in our lives. We can learn to be content through Christ who gives us strength. The verse does not read, "I can do all things through my education, my prowess, my money, my accomplishments, my friends." It does not read, "I can do all things through the power of positive thinking, through drugs and alcohol, through sexual gratification, through political position, etc." We can be satisfied in life with what God has given to us through the strength of Christ.

Learned behavior begins in the mind. Paul learned to be content by learning to think correctly. Check out Philippians 4:8. Paul commanded these Christians to think about everything that was good in life. In Greek, the word "think" is *logidzamai*, from which we derive our mathematical word logarithm. In the early seventeenth century, John Napier developed logarithms as a way to help make difficult calculations simpler. Logarithms require deep thinking. The word "think," which Paul used, is also a present tense imperative, which means that he commanded the Christians in Philippi to think continually about what is true, noble, right, pure, lovely, admirable, excellent, and praiseworthy.

For Paul, right thinking leads to right living, and the same can happen in our lives. When we dwell on the good in our lives that God gives us, we can become both grateful and content. When we are content, we are more likely to admit that we have *too much* and it is time to live with less in the land of more.

Are you and I be numbered among the "haves," meaning people who have learned to be content with what we have? Do we have right thinking which leads to right living? What if we thought deeply about all that is good, right, and admirable in our lives—could we then recognize the many ways in which God has already blessed us? In the strength of Jesus, would we be able to say, "We have learned to be content with what we have, whether living in plenty or in want"?

SKIN IN THE GAME

▲ What would a simple life look like for you? Be specific.

▲ To be content means to be satisfied. We should never be content or satisfied with our spiritual lives. On the other hand, are you satisfied with the material aspect of your life? If so, how did this happen? If not, why not?

THE NEW YOU

For decades, Americans have been intrigued with super heroes. Whether we read of them in comic books or watch them on a movie screen, super heroes have captured our attention.   In particular, super hero movies are generating hundreds of millions of dollars in revenue as we flock to theaters to watch the antics of Batman, Spiderman, Superman, Iron Man, and a host of others. Often times, the story line involves the hero experiencing a life-altering event. For example, a spider bit Peter Parker and he changed into Spider-Man. He became a new Peter Parker with super-human power. In the 2002 movie *Spider-Man*, there is an emotional scene that captures this point. Peter's Uncle Ben looks at his young nephew and tells him, "These are the years when a man becomes the man he's going to be for the rest of his life. Just be careful who you change into."[6]

"Just be careful who you change into." We may not be morphing into super heroes, but we are changing. Every single one of us undergoes change. So then, what kind of adults do we become when we leave childhood behind us? Do we become people who know how to be truly content in life, satisfied with what we have? "Be careful what you change into" is great advice.

Derek Thompson, a senior economics and labor market editor for *The Atlantic*, observed that over the past one hundred years, Americans have turned yesterday's luxury goods into today's necessities. For example, in 1900, less than one out of ten families had access to electricity or even owned a stove. In 1915, less than one out of ten families owned a car. In 1930, less than one out of ten families owned a clothes washer or refrigerator. In 1945, less than one out of ten families had air-conditioning or a clothes dryer. In 1960, less than one out of ten families owned a color television or dishwasher. In 1975, less than one out of ten families had a microwave. In 1990, less than one out of ten families had a mobile phone or internet access. Thompson concluded, "Today, at least ninety percent of the country has a stove, electricity, car, fridge, clothes washer, air-conditioning, color TV, microwave, and cell phone. They make our lives better. They might even make us happier. But they are [never] enough."[7] Have luxuries become necessities? Has the luxury of a cruise vacation now become a necessity? Has the luxury of cosmetic dentistry or surgery become a necessity? Has the luxury of that new car smell, those designer jeans, or that country-club membership become a necessity? We keep accumulating more because we do not appreciate what we already have. More is never enough. Content? Be careful what you change into.

Today there is a condition that sociologists call FOMO, which stands for the "fear of missing out." Fueled by Facebook and other social media platforms, this fear emerges when individuals read updates posted by their family and friends.

Anxiety rises when people think that others have something they do not have, or are doing something they are not doing. For example, they do not have the 3,000 square foot home with a three-stall attached garage. They are not flying out to Colorado to ski over a three-day weekend. FOMO, the fear of missing out, produces stress and anxiety in many people. As a result, people will go to great lengths to *not* miss out when it comes to having and doing much—even *too much*. Be careful what you change into.

Rick Warren is the founding pastor of Saddleback Community Church in southern California, and he is the author of *The Purpose Driven Life*. Second only to the Holy Bible, it is the most translated book in the world, appearing in over one hundred languages. It has also been on the *New York Times* best-seller list for years. Warren is a person of indescribable influence. He leads a church with more than 20,000 in attendance. He fights AIDS alongside internationally known figures like Bono. From dignitaries to presidents, he continues to impact the lives of powerful and influential people.

It's no surprise then that Rick Warren is wealthy. His book brought him overnight success and catapulted him onto an international stage. But, Warren resists being renowned—at least in a monetary sense. Over the last decade he has lived off the proceeds of his book sales and has returned all of the salary his church paid him. He refers to himself as a "volunteer pastor." In an interview with *Forbes*, Warren describes how he has learned to be content: "I drive a 12 year old Ford, have lived in the same house for the last 22 years, bought my watch at Wal-Mart, and I don't own a boat or a jet."[8] Rick Warren is being very careful of what he changes into.

Just like with my dad, I also received an inheritance from my mom. And like my dad, my mom died suddenly of a stroke. Her death caught me by surprise, but what I inherited from my mother surprised me more. You see, her early years were filled with painful events. She was an only child because her mother died giving birth to her. When she started kindergarten at the age of five, her dad committed suicide because he could not cope with his grief. Her grandmother stepped in to raise her. During the week of my mom's high school graduation, her grandmother died of a massive heart attack. In the next couple of years, my parents met, fell in love, and were married. At the wedding, my mom's uncle, who was like a father to her, gave her away. Soon after, he was diagnosed with cancer and my mom cared for him in the spare bedroom of my folks' newlywed apartment. This is where he died. Not long after his death, my mom and dad had their first baby—a little girl they named Mary. Sadly, she died shortly after birth.

By the time my mother was twenty-two years old, five significant people in her life had died. Moreover, the nature of these deaths were tragic for a young girl and wife. If anyone could have been angry with God, it was my mom. If anyone could have become bitter about life and caustic towards people, it was my mom. But, she didn't. Instead of looking at life and seeing everything that was wrong with it, my mom was optimistic and hope-filled. When I was growing up and griping about my "problems," my mom reprimanded me and reminded me that there were people in this world with *real* problems. The inheritance my mom gave me was that she taught me to look for and find everything that was good, right, excellent, and praiseworthy. Was she bitter? No. She was a far better person. She was careful of who she turned into.

An inheritance can be a funny thing. Some people hope to inherit stocks, bonds, cash, and more. Others are content with *real* treasure that cannot be measured in dollars and cents. Learn to be content.

SKIN IN THE GAME

▲ FOMO. In what ways do you struggle with the fear of missing out? Be specific.

▲ What are the things in your life you see as necessities but others would see as luxuries?

▲ What will your children and grandchildren inherit from you? Will their inheritance consist of valuable goods or good values?

Chapter 4
The Principle of Trust

"Some trust in chariots and some in horses,
but we trust in the name of the Lord our God."
Psalm 20:7

A couple of exciting events took place in 1956. First, I was born, which was pretty exciting for me. But second, our federal government adopted the motto: "In God We Trust." Within a year this phrase began appearing on all American currency. Our nation declared that we were trusting in God, and to be honest, there was a good purpose for doing so. Here's why.

Think about life in the mid-1950s. Although World War II had finally come to an end, world conflict continued. A war flared up in Korea, and another one soon began in Vietnam. These occurred in the context of a larger war that raged on without the shooting of guns or the dropping of bombs. The Cold War was being fought between two super-powers: the United States and the former Soviet Union. Two ideologies—democracy and communism—went head to head. The Soviet Union championed atheism, teaching millions of school children that God did not exist. America countered by declaring the opposite: "In God We Trust."

While international conflict raged between these two belief systems, another struggle arose quickly here at home. It involved our new national motto. "In God We Trust" became hotly debated between Americans. This conflict continues into our own day. Lawsuits have been filed against the motto's use by individuals and organizations, demanding that it be removed because it violates the establishment clause of our Constitution (i.e., that our federal government cannot establish a state religion). Every lawsuit has failed as the courts have determined that the motto does not promote nor establish a state religion.

Yet, this is not merely about a motto. This is about a way of life. This is about trust, and it is a biblical principle by which we must live if we are to be free of financial bondage. Whether we care to admit it or not, there comes a time in life when we have a hard time trusting in God. Case in point, the comedian Tim Allen does not find this issue a laughing matter in his life. When he was eleven, Allen's father died in a car accident. His dad was driving home from a college football game when he was struck and killed by a drunk driver. Nearly fifty years later, Allen shares with people how the loss of his father still affects his life, "Part of me still doesn't trust that everything will work out all right. I knew my father was dead, but I was never satisfied with why he was dead. I wanted answers that minute from God. And I've had a tumultuous relationship with my Creator ever since."[9]

Do we trust in God or not? This is a fundamental issue in life. It's one of those basic lessons that we have to learn. There comes a time in life when each one of us must learn to trust God. Take for example a guy named Elijah. We begin reading his story in 1 Kings 17 when he confronted evil King Ahab of Israel. God sent Elijah to get in the face of Israel's wicked ruler to inform him that the nation was soon to experience a serious drought. After delivering the bad news, Elijah went into the wilderness to live alongside a brook. Here, God sent ravens day after day to provide him with meat and bread to eat. Water came from the brook; meat and bread came from the ravens. Ultimately, it all came from God. Elijah was about to enter spiritual battle against the formidable Ahab, and this was his boot camp where he had to learn to trust God.

Our coins and currency declare, "In God We Trust," but do we? Can we declare the same and mean it? Have you ever had to trust God—really depend on Him? We usually trust in our jobs, our paychecks, our credit cards, our checking accounts, and more. Yet, do we realize that God is the one that really supplies us all that we have? Have we ever been without a job, a place to call home, a car to drive, or food to eat? Have we ever been at the end of our rope, not knowing how we would survive just one more day? If we're honest, many of us have been—and still are—consumed with worry because we've not learned to trust God.

Interestingly, we have learned to trust many things besides God in our modern world. Consider the elevator. How often do you or I ride in one? When we do, we can thank Elisha Otis for making it a safe ride. Otis elevators dominate the market. Although he did not invent the elevator, he invented its braking system. In their early years, elevators were not very safe, and therefore were limited to buildings no more than six stories high. But, once Otis developed the braking system, the "sky was the limit" and the era of the skyscraper was born. At first, few people bought the Otis elevator because they still considered it unsafe. To prove that his product was reliable, Otis displayed his elevator in 1854 at the Crystal Palace Exhibition in downtown Manhattan. Repeatedly, he rode his elevator high above the crowd, and with the people on edge of their seats, he gave the order to cut the rope! The elevator plunged toward the ground. But before it crashed, the brakes were applied and the elevator came to a stop, safely delivering Otis to the ground. The demonstration worked, and the Otis elevator began selling because people began to trust the creator of its brakes.[10]

When will we begin trusting our Creator? When I was a young husband and father, I often thought how would I ever be able to save enough money for a down payment on a house, which, back then, was twenty percent of the purchase price. I wondered if I would I be able to put braces on my sons' teeth when my first preaching ministry paid $100 per week and provided us with a parsonage in which to live. How would I ever be able to save enough money to put my sons through college on a preacher's salary? Moreover, where would I ever get the money needed for my own graduate and post-graduate studies? Simply put, in my early years of adulthood, I needed to go through boot camp and learn to trust God.

START DOING THIS

The disciples of Jesus went through a boot camp of their own, and their basic training involved learning to trust Jesus. One of the most powerful lessons they learned from Jesus happened in the midst of a miracle. It was the only miracle recorded in all four Gospels, and it involved a lot of food (Matthew 14:13-21; Mark 6:32-44; Luke 9:10-17; John 6:1-15).   When we read through these four accounts, we discover that Jesus fed not only five thousand men, but also women and children. There could have been as many as ten to fifteen thousand people there that day, and what a day it was! All four Gospel writers provide us with some great insights that we do not want to miss.

- **PAIN & PROBLEMS**

Notice that before Jesus performed this miracle, people were struggling. The opening verses of Matthew 14 tell us about the beheading of John the Baptist, and we are reminded that some people were grieving, including Jesus. John and Jesus were related (Luke 1:36). After Jesus learned about the execution, He withdrew by boat to a solitary place. Could it be that Jesus wanted to be alone to grieve? If so, His solitude was short-lived, because a great crowd of people followed Him on foot to where He landed on the other side of the Sea of Galilee.

As Jesus moved about in the crowd, He had compassion on them and healed their sick. The word "compassion" is a unique word, and it is used most often in the New Testament in connection with Jesus. The word is anatomical in nature and refers to the "bowel"—think large intestines. When Jesus saw hurting, disadvantaged, spiritually lost people, He had compassion on them. In other words, feelings of empathy welled up from deep within Jesus. When He saw the pain and the problems in the lives of people, He did something about it. He healed them, and then, He did something more.

As evening approached, the people grew hungry. Their stomachs were growling. Remember, first-century folks did not eat in the same manner as we do. They did not enjoy three meals a day with a bevy of snacks in between. They had one primary meal a day and it was towards the end of the day. In this remote place, these thousands upon thousands of people were all getting hungry as the day drew to a close. As well, these people had a significant hike back to their villages, and unless they ate something, it was a hike that was going to happen on empty stomachs. Hunger became just one more problem for them.

· PATTERN

The people's hunger problem quickly became a major problem for the disciples because Jesus told them to give the people something to eat. That expectation threw the disciples into a frenzy because they had no food nor the money to buy food. No one in the crowd had food, except a boy who had a "happy meal" of five loaves of bread and two fish. The text reveals that Jesus already had in mind what He was going to do, which tells us that He was about to teach His disciples a lesson. This miracle, told by all four Gospel writers, was a lesson that He never wanted them to forget.

After Jesus had the people sit down in groups of fifty and one hundred, He prayed, thanking God for the food. The fish and bread became more fish and bread. What did the people see? Did the food "bubble up" in the hands of Jesus? We don't know, but what we do know is that several thousands of people sitting around in large groups were being served by a catering crew of twelve. The disciples most likely used large baskets to carry the bread and fish to each group of people. Moreover, the text tells us that the people ate and they were satisfied. This word "satisfied" means that they could not eat another bite. It is a Greek word that refers to cattle waddling away from a feeding trough after eating all they wanted. Some people say there is always room for JELLO, but in this case, there wasn't! All of the people waddled back home.

Picture this. How many trips did the catering crew make to and from Jesus to refill their baskets? Do you see a pattern here? The disciples needed food for thousands of hungry, broken people. The disciples did not have any food to give them. But, Jesus did. Go to Jesus. Get food. Take food to hungry people. Empty the basket. Go to Jesus. Get more food. Take the food to hungry people. Empty the basket. Go to Jesus. Get more food. Take the food to hungry people. Empty the basket. There's the pattern! What the disciples needed for the hungry, problem-plagued people, they got from Jesus.

What they needed for them, they got from Him. To drive this truth home, Jesus had the disciples pick up the leftovers. The text reads that there were twelve baskets brimming over with leftover bread and fish. As each disciple gathered up a basketful of food, they realized that Jesus was the source of all that they needed. The lesson that day ended with an exclamation point!

What they needed for them, they got from Him. This truth speaks into our lives. What we need for them, we get from Him. We are surrounded by people. Some of the people we know, and for whom we care, have pain and problems. Like the disciples, we do not know how we possibly can be of help. We don't think we have the resources that it will take to help them. We default too quickly to a "can't, won't, and don't" mentality, saying, "I can't possibly help because I don't have something with which to help, so I just won't help. I won't help them anymore. I don't help people like that." The disciples protested that they didn't have food, nor money to get food, for the multitude of hungry people. No problem. Jesus did. When we protest to God that we don't have the time, talent, and treasure to help others, He says, "No problem." What we need for them, we get from Him—that is, if we turn to and trust in Him.

Mark Smith, a thirty-three-year-old lecturer at Cambridge University, capsized his kayak in treacherous waters off the Isle of Wight in England. Clinging to his boat and reaching for his cell phone, Smith's first inclination was to call his father, even though his dad was training British troops some 3,500 miles away in the nation of Dubai. Without delay, his father relayed his son's mayday call to the British Coast Guard, which had a base of operation less than a mile from Smith's location. Within twelve minutes, a helicopter rescued Smith.[11] Think this through. Smith's first inclination was to turn to and trust in his dad for a rescue. Will we do the same? When will we learn this principle of trusting in God?

Worried about putting braces on your children's teeth? Tossing and turning through the night because you don't know how you will pay for your children's college education? Struggling to keep food on the table and a roof over your family's head? What you need for them, you get from Him. Have you learned to turn to and trust in God? It is the pattern that we need to follow just as much as His disciples did.

SKIN IN THE GAME

▲ Who are the "thems" in your life? Who is counting on you to provide for them—and what do they need from you? Be specific.

▲ Recall a time in the past when you called on God. How did God come through for you? What led you to turn to and trust in Him?

▲ Jesus turned to His Father in heaven. He acknowledged that God would provide the food for thousands. Do you pray like Jesus? If not, why not?

STOP DOING THIS

If we start turning to and trusting in God, we will be able to stop doing something else, and that something else is worry. Our culture feeds on worry. Just read the morning paper or watch the evening news. We worry about an outbreak of Ebola half of a world away, and we then worry here because the media tells us it could spread to America. We worry about rising food prices because of a record-breaking drought. We worry about rising fuel costs because of a fire at a refinery. We worry about the increasing instability in the Middle East and the grow-ing aggression of Russia. We are fed a continual diet of worry. But Jesus said to stop it.

In His Sermon on the Mount, Jesus talked directly about worry (Matthew 6:25-34). Why? Worry was a front-burner issue in the first century. That's why Jesus preached about it. In driver's training, we are told to do something specific when we approach a railroad crossing. We must stop, look, and listen. If we fail to stop, look, and listen, we could collide with a train. Similarly, the same can happen when it comes to worry. Jesus told His listeners and He tells us today that if we are to conquer worry, we must stop, look, and listen.

- **STOP**

Not once, but three times, Jesus commanded people to stop worrying. He didn't suggest or advise them to stop worrying. He commanded them. The Greek grammar here means "to stop doing what you are already doing" (verses 25, 31, 34). This would have been hard for them to do. Everyday life in the an-cient world was worse than anything we know of today, even compared to life in developing nations. People lived in dark, one-room houses that typically had no windows. They were smoky because of a fire in the middle of the room, and they were damp and smelly because of a leaky roof. The odor could also get quite bad because people smelled of sweat, urine, and feces. The streets, if we can call them streets, were full of mud and human and animal waste. People would even leave human and animal corpses to rot in the streets when there were no re-sponsible people to care for the dead, whether human or animal. How could they not worry over their next meal or their next drink of clean water? How could they not worry about getting another cloak after the one they had wore out, becoming nothing more than a rag? Today, people live to work. Back then, people worked to live—to survive for one more day. Billions of people do the same today. Gary Haugen, President of International Justice Mission, describes what it means to be poor.

> "…the poor are the ones who can never afford to have any bad luck. They can't get an infection because they don't have access to any medicine. They can't get sick or miss their bus or get injured because they will lose their menial labor job if they don't show up for work. They can't misplace their pocket change because it's actually the only money they have left for food. They can't have their goats get sick because it's the only source of milk they have. On and on it goes. Of course the bad news is, everybody has bad luck. It's just that most of us have margins of resources and access to support that allow us to weather the storm, because we're not trying to live off $2.00 a day."[12]

When it comes to this definition of being poor, most of us are not truly poor, yet we worry as if we are. Worry is one of the sins we most often commit. Why? We do not trust God. Though our currency declares "In God We Trust," we don't. When we worry, we declare that God cannot be trusted and that His Word is not reliable. Start trusting. Stop worrying.

· **LOOK**

While preaching on that hillside, Jesus commanded the people to look at the birds of the air. Birds forage for food while building nests and raising their young, yet God provides for them. Jesus then asked the people a penetrating question: "Are you not much more valuable than they?" Since God cares for the birds, will He not also care for us, who have been made in His image? While the people were worrying about their clothes, Jesus commanded them to consider the lilies of the field, which are "here today and tomorrow are thrown in the fire" (Matthew 6:30). Jesus called attention to their beauty and how they adorned the grassy fields, and then posed a thought-provoking question, "Will He not much more clothe you—you of little faith?" (Matthew 6:30)

Worry is irrelevant. Getting right to the heart of the matter, Jesus asked a pointed question: "Can any one of you by worrying add a single hour to your life?" (Matthew 6:27) We are obsessed with living longer. We exercise, diet, take supplements and more, to soothe our anxiety about living long. Worry cannot give us longevity. In reality, it is a killer. It is not what we eat that kills us, but what eats at us. Medical research has shown in one study after another that worry robs us of good health. Worry produces a litany of medical problems: acid reflux, chest pains, ulcers, sleep disorders, high blood pressure, and more. We spend hundreds of millions of dollars on medications to help us and heal us of worry. Moreover, worry is irreverent. Worry is not trusting God in the present when He has been so faithful in the past. Start trusting. Stop worrying.

· **LISTEN**

At the very heart in this portion of His sermon, Jesus said something that they needed to hear. He wanted them, and us, to listen. Here it is. Jesus said that God-followers should first seek His Kingdom and His righteousness. Instead of pursuing the world and all the stuff it has to offer, "seek first His kingdom and His righteousness" (Matthew 6:33). The word kingdom does not mean a geographical territory. It is a spiritual kingdom. As Christian scholar Dallas Willard explains, God's Kingdom is "the range of His effective will, where what He wants is done."[13]

Listen! Jesus tells us to bring our little kingdoms under God's Kingdom. We must allow God to have dominion over us. We must surrender to His rule in our lives— even over our money and the things that money can buy.

At the beginning of this section on worry, Jesus used the word "therefore," which calls attention to what preceded it (Matthew 6:25). Just before commanding people to stop worrying, Jesus preached that no one can serve two masters. It is impossible to serve both God and money. The word money means more than just currency. It refers to all that money can buy. We often obsess over our possessions. When we give an excessive amount of attention to our stuff, our stuff has our attention. We fret. We stew. We worry. We do the very thing Jesus commanded us not to do. Start trusting. Stop worrying.

Google is not only an internet search engine. As a company, Google is impacting our culture and revealing some interesting facts about the words we use and the things we value. Because Google has now digitized thirty million books, we have access to a lot of data that gives us a view of ourselves from thirty-six thousand feet. Author Christian Rudder explains: "This body of data has created a new field of quantitative cultural studies called culturomics; its primary method is to track changes in word use through time. The long reach of the data (it goes back to 1800) allows an unusual look at people and what's important to them."[14] For example, shortly after General Electric introduced the icebox, the word "ice cream" became popular. You see, a study of our vocabulary and individual word usage indicates what is important to us. A study of the name "God" reveals a steady decline in its use for the past decades. The name God is now only used roughly one-third as often in American writing as it was in the early nineteenth century.

This is a cultural phenomenon, but it may be more. It may indicate that we are growing less focused on God. We may be failing to turn to and trust in God. What will it take for us to say, "In God we trust," and really mean it?

SKIN IN THE GAME

▲ I worry. I play the "what if" game very well. Do you? How often and over what do you worry?

▲ Can you spot fear and worry in the news? What news stories fuel worry and anxiety in you and others?

▲ How do we insult God with our worry?

Chapter 5
The Principle of Humility

"Humble yourselves, therefore, under God's mighty hand
that He may lift you up in due time. Cast all your anxiety on Him
because He cares for you."
1 Peter 5:6-7

When we are not feeling well, we make a trip to the doctor. Once diagnosed, our treatment may involve a combination of things: physical therapy, prescription drugs, a special diet, and more. When we pursue this treatment combination, we embark on a journey to improved health. Each element of our treatment works with the other to help us achieve good health. They work together. They are inseparable. Each is essential.

The same is true when we are financially ill. Consider the symptoms: late payments, no savings, maxed-out credit cards, overdrawn checking accounts, poor credit scores, mountains of debt, no tithing or giving, etc. To become financially healthy, we must embrace four biblical principles that work together: gratitude, contentment, trust, and humility. You see, we will never experience financial health until we are truly *grateful* to God for His provision in our lives. We will never be grateful until we are *content* with what we have, whether living with little or with much. We will never be content until we have learned to *trust* God and His care for us. We will never trust God until we *humble* ourselves before God, admitting our need for Him. These four principles work together. They are inseparable. Each is essential.

The journey to financial health involves a journey into humility, like the one frequently made by high-wire artist and devoted Christian, Nik Wallenda. Wallenda's daredevil feats, such as walking a tightrope across Niagara Falls and the Grand Canyon, have been witnessed by millions of people around the world. When he has accomplished such feats, cheering fans have wanted his autograph and picture. Knowing his temptation for pride, Wallenda does something to intentionally disengage arrogant thinking. After the media and crowds leave, he picks up their trash. Wallenda recently wrote:

> "My purpose is simply to help clean up after myself. The huge crowd left a great deal of trash behind, and I feel compelled to pitch in. Besides, after the inordinate amount of attention I sought and received, I need to keep myself grounded. Three hours of cleaning up debris is good for my soul. Humility does not come naturally to me. So if I have to force myself into situations that are humbling, so be it …. I know that I need to get down on my hands and knees like everyone else. I do it because it's a way to keep from tripping. As a follower of Jesus, I see Him washing the feet of others. I do it because if I don't serve others I'll be serving nothing but my ego."[15]

Nik Wallenda deliberately moves in the direction of humility. A journey to financial health demands a journey into humility. Our pride fuels us to purchase what we do not need with money we do not have to impress people we do not know. Pride pushes us to depend on creditors to fund our out-of-control spending and entices us to ignore our Creator, who is also our Sustainer. To be financially healthy, each of us must embark on a journey to humility.

A JOURNEY WITH A DESTINATION

Jesus made such a journey. There came a time when Jesus deliberately moved into humility. The Apostle Paul described this journey in a rich and powerful way in his letter to the church in Philippi.

Philippians 2:6-8

Your attitude should be the same as that of Christ Jesus: Who, being in very nature God, did not consider equality with God something to be used to his own advantage; rather He *made Himself nothing* by taking the very nature of a servant, being made in human likeness. And being found in appearance as a man, He *humbled* Himself by becoming obedient to death—even death on a cross! (italics mine)

This passage describes *the* defining moment of the most defining person in history. There never was—nor will there ever be—anyone like Jesus Christ. Though He was fully God, Jesus *humbled* Himself. He took a journey into humility. Humble means "to lower oneself." It is a place to which someone goes. Jesus chose to forgo His status of being equal with God to journey into a humble existence here on earth.

Cameras flash when a baby is born. A birth is a Kodak moment. In much the same way, the birth of Jesus was a Kodak moment, and it included one snapshot of humility after another. Even though Jesus was fully and completely God,

He was born to a peasant girl from an obscure village. His adoptive earthly father was a blue-collar worker, a carpenter by trade. The Son of God was born out in a barn and laid in a feeding trough for animals. Shepherds—those who were reviled by most people—were the first people to come calling on Baby Jesus in the delivery room. Think about this. Jesus Christ, the Creator of Life, was born into and confined by a human body. Jesus, the Sustainer of all the universe, became a helpless infant. Jesus entered this world and began His journey into humility.

Pictures of humility continued throughout His life. Jesus healed those who were ill. He fed those who were hungry. He raised people from the dead. He defended women and welcomed children. He even washed the feet of His disciples. He was not made famous by owning a home or writing a book. His resume did not include a college degree or an elected office. While on earth, Jesus moved into humility.

Even in His death, Jesus was humble. Though He was—and still is—righteous God, Jesus allowed Himself to be arrested and stand trial as a common criminal. Though He was—and still is—holy God, Jesus died for sins He did not commit. Though He was—and still is—eternal God, Jesus experienced physical death. Crucifixion was both horrific and humiliating. While Jesus hung naked on the cross, the Roman soldiers gambled for the last thing He owned: the clothing He wore the day He died. Once dead, He was buried in a borrowed tomb. Jesus moved into humility.

When Jesus embarked on the journey into humility, He first *made Himself nothing.* This is from a Greek word meaning "to empty." It is a rare word appearing only five times in the New Testament, and those instances are exclusively in Paul's writings. A popular interpretation of this word states that Jesus emptied Himself of deity while He was on earth. Yet, that interpretation is incorrect. The Apostle Paul wrote that in Jesus, the fullness of the deity dwells in bodily form (Colossians 2:9). While living on the earth, Jesus was completely God. He did not empty Himself of His deity. Philippians 2 does not tell us *what* Jesus emptied Himself of, but it does tell us *how* He did it.

Jesus made Himself nothing. He put on flesh and became a servant. He emptied Himself of title and status. He emptied Himself when He did not demand honor, rank, or privilege. When confronting His disciples of their pride, Jesus told them that He had come to serve and not to be served (Mark 10:35-45). Jesus emptied Himself of following His own will for His life. The night before He died, Jesus submitted His will to that of God's—"Yet not as I will, but as you will" (Matthew 26:39-44). The Apostle Paul described this well when he wrote: "...for your sake He became poor, so that through His poverty you might become rich" (2 Corinthians 8:9). Though He was entitled to all of the privileges of being fully and completely God, Jesus emptied Himself of His status and claim to heaven's riches.

Jesus made a deliberate decision to give and not to get, to serve and not be served, to submit and not to dominate. Jesus chose to make a journey to a most humble destination.

SKIN IN THE GAME

▲ How do you move into humility? Be specific.

▲ Have you humbly admitted your need for God? In humility, do ycu admit that God is your Creator and Sustainer?

▲ Jesus paid for people to experience eternal life. How did He pay physically? How did He pay emotionally? How did He pay spiritually?

A JOURNEY WITH A DETOUR

Instead of moving in the direction of humility, pride becomes a familiar detour in all of our lives. Pride is a recurring problem for us, and it is at the heart of our financial struggles. From the moment of birth, a baby cries to be fed, to be changed, and to be held. A baby cries because a baby wants something. When the baby begins to grow, we anxiously await hearing his or her first words: "Mama, Dada." Yet, it's not long before a toddler learns—and uses—the word, "Mine!" "Mine," is screamed over and again as the toddler wants what another toddler has. The trouble is, we struggle to outgrow this behavior. As adults, we want what others have: a bigger house, a newer car, expensive clothing, exciting travel, and more. What began as a survival instinct when we were infants grows into a full-fledged obsession with self. Just as babies cry for attention, we want the attention of people around us, whether we know them or not. We want to turn heads in our direction by what we have and do.

Just as we learned "stop-look-listen" in driver's ed, I recall another lesson from class. Another rule of the road is that when passing a car on the road – don't look at it. My teacher said that if you look at the car you are passing, you will begin steering in that direction. You will have a tendency to drift towards that car. Come to think of it, this rule of the road is true when it comes to our personal finances.

While driving past a new sub-division under construction, you veer towards it—wanting to build a custom home among all the others. When someone walks past you in designer jeans, you want a pair. When someone parks next to you in his new Jeep Wrangler Rubicon, you want one—but in a different color. Something or someone captures our attention, and we begin drifting in that direction. Companies are experts at getting our attention. Using slick ads in magazines, too-good-to-be-true deals on the internet, and clever commercials on television, our thinking quickly drifts in their direction. Before you know it, we soon find ourselves buying something we don't need with money we don't have to impress people we don't know. Why? Something or someone captures our attention; we drift in that direction, and pride fuels our purchase.

Pride becomes our promoter. We self-promote. Just as there is such a thing as good cholesterol and bad cholesterol, there is such a thing as good self-promotion and bad self-promotion. When looking for a job, we need to do some good self-promotion in hopes of landing the position. We update our resume and sharpen our interviewing skills in hopes of getting the job. There is a good side of self-promotion.

On the other hand, the bad kind of self-promotion is a killer, and it becomes part of our thinking at an early age. We begin each day thinking, "Mirror,

mirror, on the wall, who's the fairest of them all?" Every morning, we get up and look in the mirror. We primp. We fixate on looking good, and this drive is fueled by a multi-billion dollar health and beauty industry. The obsession begins at a young age. For example, the TLC cable network television show *Toddlers & Tiaras* features preschoolers competing in beauty pageants. Is this a new normal for little girls in our culture? Starting in childhood, we begin climbing on the pedestal of self-promotion for all to see. We want to turn people's heads in our direction. We've taken the detour of pride.

Hollywood lives this way. I'm old enough to remember the day when the one and only popular award show was the Oscars. But in recent years, the list of award shows has grown in popularity to include the Emmys, the Grammys, the Country Music Awards, the People's Choice Awards, the Golden Globe awards, and the Young Hollywood awards, just to name a few. In addition to the award shows, movie stars are immortalized by having his or her "star" laid in concrete along the Walk of Fame.

It happens among professional athletes. Billionaire owners have franchises worth staggering sums of money, and players earn multi-million dollar paychecks. Actors and athletes have something in common—an agent. The agent promotes his or her clients so that they stay in the limelight and receive much more than mere attention.

Most of us don't have an agent or promoter. We promote ourselves, and we do it well. We mention ourselves in conversations using those ever-popular pronouns of "me, myself, and I." When listening to someone tell their story, we interrupt with our own story and we make certain that it is both bigger and better.

We make ourselves look and appear more successful than we really are. We draw attention to ourselves and away from others. We like being needed. We do such a good job of promoting ourselves that we don't need an agent or a promoter.

We need to understand something: self-promoting leads to self-destruction. Living this way can crush the life out of us as we try to be first in the line of life, out in front of everyone else. Proverbs 16:18 says that pride goes before destruction and a haughty spirit before a fall. James 4:6 teaches us that God opposes the proud but gives grace to the humble. What would it be like to have God against us? God opposes us when we promote ourselves. Self-promotion leads to self-destruction! Just before His death by crucifixion, Jesus said, "For those who exalts themselves will be humbled, and those who humble themselves will be exalted" (Matthew 23:12). That is exactly what happened to Jesus. Jesus humbled Himself and God exalted Him (Philippians 2:9). Don't take the detour of pride!

Remember, Jesus emptied Himself of status. Status is ingrained in our culture. It is a natural part of our thinking. We organize daily life around status. We have titles at work, officer ranks in the military, grading systems and degrees in education, starting teams in athletics, balance sheets in big business, offices within politics, and more. Status even appears on a person's Facebook page. Status can feed a person's ego. When our status is higher at work, we can become prideful. When we have achieved educational status, we risk becoming arrogant. With status so embedded in our lives, how do we "empty ourselves"? How do we go on a journey to a lower place called humility?

While on earth, Jesus had rank and privilege because He was fully God (Colossians 2:9). While on earth, He was the Master Physician and Master Teach-

er, having unlimited skill and ability. While on earth, He had access to indescribable wealth and resources; after all, "the earth is the Lord's and everything in it"
(Psalm 24:1). Yet, while on earth, Jesus restrained Himself, moving to a place of
profound humility.

Do you and I have rank and privilege? Rank may involve our position at
work, our team at school, or our favored position in the family or with friends. But
is humility evident in our lives? Do you and I have skill and ability? We may have
a degree, intellect, significant skills, and more, but is humility evident in our lives?
Are we people of wealth and means? We are if we can go to McDonalds and buy
a happy meal, because that is something two-thirds of the world cannot do. But
even with wealth and means, how is humility evident in our lives?

Humility is not thinking less of ourselves, but thinking less often of ourselves. Humility is putting others before us and their needs before ours. Humility
is thinking more highly of others than we think of ourselves. Humility is not something done to us, but something that we do. It is the kind of person we become as
we follow the example of Jesus.

St. Francis of Assisi, Italian Monk (1181-1226) and Rafael Merry del Val
(1865-1930) are credited for writing the following prayer. Take time to often–and
sincerely–say this prayer because prayer is a powerful weapon against pride.

O Jesus, meek and humble of heart, hear me.

From the desire of being esteemed, deliver me, Jesus.

From the desire of being loved, deliver me, Jesus.

From the desire of being praised, deliver me, Jesus.

From the desire of being preferred to others, deliver me, Jesus.

From the desire of being consulted, deliver me, Jesus.

From the desire of being approved, deliver me, Jesus.

From the fear of being humiliated, deliver me, Jesus.

From the fear of being despised, deliver me, Jesus.

From the fear of being rebuked, deliver me, Jesus.

From the fear of being criticized, deliver me, Jesus.

From the fear of being forgotten, deliver me, Jesus.

From the fear of being ridiculed, deliver me, Jesus.

From the fear of being wronged, deliver me, Jesus.

From the fear of being suspected, deliver me, Jesus.

That others may be loved more than I,

Jesus, grant me the grace to desire it.

That others may be esteemed more than I,

Jesus, grant me the grace to desire it.

That in the opinion of the world others may

increase and I may decrease,

Jesus, grant me the grace to desire it.

That others may be chosen and I set aside,

Jesus, grant me the grace to desire it.

Amen.

Author and business leader Ken Blanchard has coined a phrase that caught my attention. Some years ago, I attended a leadership conference where he taught about the acronym E.G.O.—"Edging God Out." When we journey on the road of life and we take a detour towards pride, we edge God out of our lives. The detour is marked EGO. When this happens, God no longer plays an important role in our lives, let alone the starring role. We save that role for ourselves.

Money problems are deeply rooted in a heart of pride. Once we realize this truth and we do an about-face, moving into a place of humility, our financial health can begin to improve. It requires a surrendered life to Jesus, staying focused on the destination of humility, and refusing to take the detour towards pride.

Stay the course.

SKIN IN THE GAME

▲ Jesus emptied Himself of status. What status do you have? Where do you have that status—work, school, family, etc.? How can you empty yourself of that status? Be specific.

▲ How do you empty yourself of fame in order to make Jesus Christ the Famous One in your life? Be specific.

▲ Would you do any of the following to think of others before yourself?

- Let others go in front of you in the check-out lane.

- Return shopping carts for someone else out in a parking lot.

- Let others go in front of you in rush hour traffic.

- Do simple acts of service for others in the family.

- Tell someone how important they are at work.

- Compliment the abilities of others.

- Send a note of appreciation to someone who least expects it.

Chapter 6
The Plus Sign

"In fact, this is love for God: to keep His commands.
And His commands are not burdensome."
1 John 5:3

Leah and I have six young grandchildren. When our family is all together, we have some favorite games that we play, like those of Go Fish and Scrabble. Like it or not, people play games, and one favorite is Tug of War.

Do you remember playing it (or maybe still do)? I played it just a few months ago at a gathering of high school students at The Creek. A large tarp was laid on the ground with a heavy, long rope stretching in equal lengths across it, and the tarp was covered with pudding! Students went sliding into a combination of chocolate and vanilla pudding!

We play Tug of War each and every day that we live. It's a game that Christians play. How so? The Apostle Paul described the game well. He said he knew the good that he ought to do, but he didn't do it. Instead, he did the evil that was rooted deep within him (Romans 7:19-25). Day after day, Paul was tempted by evil desires within him and he confessed to giving in to them. Good and evil tugged against one another. Moreover, Paul went on to write that Jesus Christ saved him from his wretched ways, and he was given strength for the daily battles through the Holy Spirit, who raised Jesus from the dead (Romans 8:9-11).

When it comes to our finances, we play Tug of War regularly. Do we save money out of the paycheck or spend it? Do we buy a new car even though we've no yet paid for our existing car? Do we give a full tithe to the local church or a portion of a tithe? Do we buy more house than we can afford or not? Do we get another credit card and transfer the balance or not? All too often, our financial health is in critical condition—or even on life support—because we have been pulled in the wrong direction by evil desires within us. Yes, evil desires. We know that the decisions we have made financially are not sound, and they're certainly not based on Scripture.

Charlie Steinmetz had one of the greatest minds as an electrical engineer. Steinmetz built the great generators for Henry Ford to power his first manufacturing plant in Dearborn, Michigan. Once the assembly line was up and operating, it produced cars and money for Ford. One day, without warning, the assembly line stopped and the plant went dark. One mechanic after another failed to get the generators back on line, so Steinmetz was called in to remedy the problem. After doing a quick assessment, he made a correction, threw the main switch, and the plant roared back to life. The engineer sent a bill to Henry Ford for $10,000, which was a sizeable sum in the early 1900s. Ford was stunned at the amount and he sent the bill back to Steinmetz with a note questioning the excessive amount. Steinmetz responded by sending Ford a new invoice that read, "For tinkering around on the generators: $10. For knowing where to tinker: $9,990. Total Due $10,000."[16] Henry Ford paid the bill. The Holy Spirit knows where to tinker in our lives; and when we sense that the financial decisions we are making are wrong, the Holy Spirit convicts us. He is tugging at us to stop what is wrong and start what is right! He is waiting for us to turn to Him for the power to resist financial temptations and missteps. The Holy Spirit reminds us of what we have been taught in the Scriptures (John 14:26). If we are to heal our financial problems, we must do what the Word says.

The four biblical principles—gratitude, contentment, trust, and humility—are vitally important, but they cannot stand alone. To them, we must add right, daily behavior. If we are to experience *real* profit, the equation needs both principles and practices functioning together. Think about the sign we use for addition and what it communicates. The plus (+) sign is an operation, a function. The principles of gratitude, contentment, trust, and humility can, and must, be acted upon. James said it succinctly: "Do not merely listen to the Word and so deceive yourselves. Do what it says" (James 1:22). The next four chapters will explore four vitally important financial practices that are rooted in the Word, and we must "do them," not merely listen to them.

Think about it. In John 9:1-7, Jesus met a man who was born blind. Jesus spat on the ground and made some mud with His saliva. He then put the mud on the man's eyes and told him to go and wash in the Pool of Siloam. The man did as Jesus commanded and he was healed! For the first time in his life, the man was able to see. Here's the important question for you and me: could Jesus have healed the man on the spot? Could He have snapped His fingers, said the word, thought the thought, and healed the man? Certainly. Do not miss this point. Jesus required the man to make an effort in order to receive the blessing. He had to do what Jesus said in order to see again.

Jesus did the same with some lepers. In Luke 17:11-14, ten lepers approached Jesus for healing. Jesus told them to go and show themselves to the priests, and as they went, they were healed. Again, here's the important question for you and me: could Jesus have healed the men? Could He have snapped His fingers, said the word, thought the thought, and the men be healed? Certainly.

Again, don't miss this point. Jesus required the lepers to make an effort to receive the blessing of their healing. They had to do what Jesus said in order to have their flesh restored.

There's an important rule of thumb when it comes to interpreting Scripture, and that rule states: if something is repeated, it's important. When something appears over and over again in Scripture—whether it be a phrase, a word, an action, or more—it should stand out to us. God wants us to notice something. In this case, it is that you and I have to make an effort to do what the Word says about money, possessions, and status if we are to receive the blessing of financial healing. So, as we move into the next chapters of *Too Much*, is it too much for the Lord to ask each of us: "Will you merely listen to My Word, or will you do it?" If we have dug a money pit into which we have fallen, we have to do our part to climb out of that pit.

I grew up in Michigan where people do "peephole" driving. People who lived in the frozen north have likely been peephole drivers a time or two. Peephole driving happens after a night of snowfall and plummeting temperatures. In the morning, because we are in a hurry to get to work or school, we scrape a small opening in the ice and snow that encases the windshield. We start the car and turn up the defroster, but it throws more frigid air against the glass. So, we keep wiping the personal-pizza-size circle above the steering wheel with our hands. We carefully drive down the snow-covered street, peering out of our peephole at other drivers peering back at us through their peepholes. Peephole driving in the winter is an apt picture of what it's like to go through life with a limited vision and understanding of the Bible.

Too many of us move through life with a limited knowledge of the Word of God. How can we do the Word if we do not know the Word? How can we improve our money problems when we have a problem knowing and living out the Word of God? We must never conform the Word to fit our lives, but rather, conform our lives to the unchanging Word of God. If our money-related problems are to become a thing of the past, we must begin thinking and living in new ways. We must not be conformed any longer to the pattern of this world. We are to be transformed by the renewing of our minds. The way we think is the way we act—especially when it comes to money.

One more thing. If the way we manage our money is to conform to the Word, we cannot listen to the wrong voices. Believe me. There will be people who will discourage you and me from doing the right thing when it comes to money and the things that money can buy. It's been happening since the opening pages of the Bible.

There was a time when Moses did some mountain climbing on Mt. Sinai. While he was on his hike, the Israelites asked Aaron to make gods—basically, idols—for them. Aaron, the "senior minister" of the Israelites, did not think twice. He told them to give him their gold earrings. He used these to make an idol of gold in the shape of a calf. When he finished it, Aaron gave it to the people and declared that this was the god who brought the Israelites out of Egypt (Exodus 32:1-6).

Whenever I read or hear that text, I ask: "Aaron, what were you thinking? How could you do this?" Aaron was the high priest, the senior minister, the chairman of the elders, the spiritual leader of God's people. What was he thinking? It had just been a matter of days since they heard the voice of God declare the Ten Commandments in Exodus 20, which begins with a strict prohibition on making idols. It had only been three months since they were freed from slavery in Egypt (Ex. 19:1). Had Aaron already forgotten the ten miraculous plagues that God brought against Egypt—plagues that Aaron personally witnessed? Had Aaron already forgotten how God divided the Red Sea; or how water, manna, and quail were provided for them? A golden calf did none of those things. God—and God alone—brought millions of Israelites out of Egypt. When Moses returned from the mountain and saw the commotion taking place among the people, he asked Aaron, "What did these people do to you that you led them into such great sin?" (Exodus 32:21). Aaron listened to the wrong voices. The spiritual leader of the people succumbed to what is so common—the powerful influence of wrong voices.

It happened to a king's son. A bit further into the Old Testament, King Solomon's son, Rehoboam, took the throne following his father's death. A painful story is told in 1 Kings 12:1-15 of how Rehoboam listened to the wrong voices. He followed the advice of his young friends, and Israel was thrown into a great civil war that divided the country and brought death and destruction to the people of God for centuries. And why? He listened to the wrong voices.

You see, if it happened to Aaron and Rehoboam, it can happen to us. When you and I decide to take decisive action to bring order to our finances, people may discourage us. When we decide to pay off debt as quickly as possible, others may not share the same thinking. When we decide to pay cash in an attempt to end an addiction to credit-cards, others may not be ready to do so. When we decide to tithe on our income and to become even more generous with God, people may think we've lost our minds. Friends, siblings, parents, even spouses may try to talk us out of hearing and obeying the Word of God. Do not listen to the wrong voices. Listen to the voice of God. Ultimately, the only way you and I can take the four biblical principles of gratitude, contentment, trust, and humility, and add them to intentional practices is if we know His Word and listen to His voice each and every day.

SKIN IN THE GAME

▲ How well do you know the Word of God? Can you recall what it teaches about money and the things money can buy? Share some of those verses with a friend or family member.

▲ If you do not know the Bible, how often do you read the Bible? What could you do to make the Word a vital part of your life? Who can hold you accountable to learning and living the Scriptures, especially when it comes to personal finances? Be specific.

Chapter 7
The Practice of Debt-Free Living

"Let no debt remain outstanding, except the
continuing debt to love one another, for whoever loves others
has fulfilled the law."
Romans 13:8

It's called the Duck Syndrome. Many people live with it. Have you ever noticed that when you watch a duck on a lake, it appears to glide along? Yet, underneath the water, it frantically paddles. People live the same way. On the surface, they appear to be happy and successful; but underneath, they are frantically attempting to keep their heads above water—particularly when it comes to their finances.

It looks like we are living the good life. We live in custom-built homes, drive new cars, wear designer clothes, have season tickets to our favorite teams, take the kids to exciting vacation destinations, and more. To others, it looks like we are well-off. But, in reality, far too many people are financing a well-to-do lifestyle with debt—and lots of it. We frantically try to stay current with payments on the house, the car, the credit cards, the student loan, and even the home equity line. If we are past due on obligations, we're paddling like crazy. If collection agencies are contacting us, we're desperately paddling away. People with too much debt look like ducks. It's called the Duck Syndrome.

Before we venture too far into this issue, I want you to know that I know a thing or two about debt. My undergraduate degree was in a finance-related field, and I worked as a lender in the banking industry before going to seminary and becoming a minister. While working in the banks, I managed the student loan portfolio, wrote commercial and home mortgages, established commercial and agricultural operating lines of credit, and processed many consumer loans before the Tax Reform Act of 1986 eliminated tax deductions for consumer loan interest. I know about debt—how people apply for it, receive it, and drown in it when they have too much of it. Debt can make people act like ducks.

Our duck-like behavior is widespread. As mentioned in Chapter One— there is a *real* problem with macro-sized debt in our federal government, as well as in a number of state and municipal governments. As I am typing this sentence, our federal debt is in excess of $18 trillion and is increasing exponentially each minute. The United States is the number one debtor nation on the face of the earth. No other country has amassed a debt the size of ours. I remember well the day when our federal debt hit the $1 trillion mark. Ronald Reagan was president, and I was twenty-five years old. It took a mere thirty-five years for our debt to increase to a staggering $18 trillion. If we do not come to grips with our debt addiction as a nation, there will come a day when the taxes we pay will not be sufficient to pay the interest on the debt. We will be insolvent. And this will be a massive problem because our government funds the budget—and budget deficits—with ever-burgeoning debt. This can also be said of many businesses, school systems, and even ministries as they struggle with debt.

So then, it should not surprise us that on a micro-scale, debt is also impacting the lives of individuals. After the Great Recession of 2008, we would have assumed that debt would have decreased. That could not be further from reality. If we check any number of resources, we quickly discover that Americans owe more now than before or during the Great Recession. Didn't we learn anything from the school-of-hard-knocks? *Money* magazine reports, "More Americans are retiring in the red. Not so long ago 'debt' was a four-letter word when spoken in the same breath as 'retirement.' Before waltzing into their golden years, Americans paid off their loans, then celebrated by burning their mortgage. How things have changed! Now a third of folks 65 and older have a mortgage...with a median balance of $56,000. Meanwhile, seniors 65 and up carry an average $10,235 on credit cards..."[17] Even those of us 55 and older can act like ducks. There is no need for me to include statistics on mortgages, credit cards, student loans, as they change too rapidly and will be out of date as soon as you finish reading this book. But the one thing that is certain about the statistics is that they will only become worse because we practice wrong thinking when it comes to debt.

WRONG THINKING LEADS TO WRONG LIVING

How did we start acting like ducks? What makes us want to appear successful, living the good life, only to be living frantically beneath the surface, struggling to keep our debt payments current? Why do we choose to live this way? Our wrong thinking can be summarized with the acronym D.E.B.T.

D FOR DESIRES

Did you ever listen to the English rock band Queen? In 1989, they wrote a song entitled "I Want it All," and the lyrics describe our behavior. The chorus lyrics repeat over and over again, declaring: "I want it all, I want it all, I want it all, and I want it now."[18] That's the mindset of far too many Americans. We have no sense of self-control. That's why we are in debt – we want it all and we want it now! Many millennials want now what took their parents decades to accumulate. We see what someone else has, or does, and we want the same—now.

E FOR ENTITLEMENT

President Lyndon Johnson introduced more than entitlement programs when he ushered in his Great Society in the 1960s. He helped birth entitlement thinking. We think we deserve the best—and the most. We act like we are entitled to living the American dream. When we think that we are entitled to the good life, it often comes at a great cost. When we make the American Dream come true with purchases paid for with debt, the dream can quickly become a nightmare. Entitlement thinking fuels debt.

B FOR BIGGER AND BETTER

We are in debt because we want what is bigger and better. We buy the latest and greatest piece of technology because what we have is not fast enough or good enough. When we buy the latest smart phone, we need the bigger data package to go with it. We buy a tablet, and then we buy a case, accessories and applications to go with it. We buy a large screen-*ultra* high definition smart television, and then we buy a cable or direct TV package to go with it. We do the same with the clothes we wear, the cars we drive, and the homes in which we live. There's always something bigger and better, and to have it—we borrow even bigger dollars.

T FOR TAUGHT

All too often, we do what we've been taught. It may be that we had parents who struggled with debt, or we had relatives and friends who lived with the Duck Syndrome—appearing to have it together, but beneath the surface they frantically tried to keep it together financially. When the government cannot pass a balanced budget amendment or operate within its budget, why should we? When we consider the example set by our debt-ridden government, along with that of our family and friends, it's no wonder that we think a debt-driven life is normal. Trust me, it isn't. There are poor examples all around us—and we follow examples. Break the cycle of debt in your family. Don't let your children buy into this lie. Teach them these principles and practices.

Christian financial author, the late Larry Burkett, said: "Debt is not normal in any economy and shouldn't be normal for God's people, regardless of how 'right' our culture might want it to seem today. We live in a debt-ridden society that is now virtually dependent on a constant expansion of credit to keep the economy going. That is symptomatic of a society no longer willing to follow God's directions."[19] Debt is not normal, and we desperately need a new normal.

SKIN IN THE GAME

▲ Does the Duck Syndrome describe you or your family? How about your business or organization? Be specific.

▲ Consider D.E.B.T. Which of these four elements are a part of your thinking—and to what degree? How are you trying to prevent your children from this wrong thinking about debt?

RIGHT THINKING LEADS TO RIGHT LIVING

When we change our thinking, we change the way we live. This is a biblical truth. In Greek, the word "repent" is a compound word formed by two words: "change" and "mind." When we repent, we change the way we live. That happens when we change the way we think. We need to change the way we think about debt or we will never change the way we live with debt.

If you have a serious interest in physical fitness, you know what it means to get in the zone. You exercise to raise your pulse—and keep it there for a certain period of time—so that your heart becomes stronger. People do cardio and strength training to become healthier. Both of my parents died of a stroke, so I know the same could possibly happen to me. For years, I've tried to be proactive in staying as healthy as possible. I've run a few marathons, a number of half-marathons, and climbed many peaks over 14,000 feet. A group of us even climbed Africa's Mt. Kilimanjaro. To do so, I have to take physical fitness seriously.

The same is true if we want to be free of those extra pounds we carry around. We may look in the mirror and admit, "Hey, it's time to trim down." What do we do to trim down? Two things come immediately to my mind: diet and exercise. Dieting is going without a certain amount of food—particularly foods that do us more harm than good. Exercise is putting in that extra effort to drop a few pounds. So, we run, swim, cycle, walk, lift weights, and more. We sweat. If we hope to trim down, there comes a time when we have to 1) go without and 2) get going.

Instead of physical fitness, let's think fiscal fitness. Far too many people are weighed down with too much debt. They don't carry around excess pounds as much as they carry around excess debt. To trim down and become more fiscally healthy, two things have to happen: diet and exercise. To become fiscally fit, we must discontinue going into debt and decrease what debt we have. It will not be easy, but it can be exciting to experience this new normal.

When we try to trim down and drop a few pounds, we must STOP eating too much food and too much of the wrong food. To trim down our debt, we must STOP borrowing money, particularly the wrong kind of money (i.e., high interest credit card debt, etc.). A number of businesses try to get people to make impulse purchases. The check-out lane is bordered on both sides with items easily purchased on impulse. While waiting to check out, we thumb through the items surrounding us, and a number of them make it into the basket. Yet, what happens when we make big-ticket impulse purchases – the kind that can only be paid for with credit?

We see signs that read: "Finance Here!" "Buy Here—Pay Here!" "0% Financing Available!" "Six Months Same as Cash!" "Buy Now—Pay Later!" When you see the sign on the truck windshield that reads: "$3,500 in Rebates," remember that you have to spend tens of thousands of dollars on that truck to get the rebate. Here are three practical rules to help you put on the brakes when it comes to big-ticket impulse buying. Leah and I made these rules early in our marriage.

Rule #1: Ask: "Do I really need this, or do I just want this?" Don't just ask this question by thinking it silently in the mind. Ask the question out loud! While standing in front of the new vehicle, the new home model, the new television, or the new whatever, turn to your spouse and ask, "Do we need this, or do we just want this?" Think twice—or even three times—before buying this big-ticket item with increased debt. The Apostle Paul tells us of a great promise: "And my God will meet all your needs according to the riches of His glory in Christ Jesus" (Philippians 4:19). Paul didn't say that God would meet all of our wants and wishes, but that He would meet our needs. We must do a gut-check when it comes to wants and needs. How much is enough when it comes to square feet under the roof, clothes in the closet, food in the freezer, vacations on the calendar, and more? What is a want and what is a need? Some individuals are head over heels in debt because they keep buying what they want, and not what they need. Moreover, Paul teaches us in the verse that it's GOD who meets our needs, not the credit card company or the big bank. Do we wait on and trust in God to provide or not? STOP signing your name on the dotted line for more debt.

Rule #2: Establish a solo-spending ceiling. Early in our marriage, Leah and I agreed that we would not make a purchase of $200 or more without discussing it with each other. If it cost more than $200, I would not buy that mower or snow blower without first talking it over with Leah. This rule has helped prevent us from making big-ticket purchases, especially when we were first starting out in marriage. After thirty-seven years of marriage, we have increased that spending ceiling, but the rule still stands. We talk before we spend large sums of money.

Rule #3: Wait. We never make a big-ticket purchase in the immediate moment. A car purchase happens only after much research, discussion, and prayer. Only then do we make a trip to the car lots and begin the buying process. Some years ago, a salesman was in our home, trying to sell us new vinyl windows that would replace the vinyl windows we had previously installed. We kept telling him that we would not make a decision that day, but he didn't take us seriously. He kept trying to sweeten the deal by throwing in a new window for free, a better coating on the glass, etc., but we kept saying that we wanted time to think and talk about it. He left angry, and without a sale, but we obeyed our rule and saved thousands of dollars by replacing only the few windows that needed replacing. Put in place some rules—safeguards—that will STOP you from signing on the dotted line and increasing your debt. To trim down and drop debt, we must diet and go without.

Remember, it's diet and exercise that are required to trim down. Likewise, it's both discontinuing debt and decreasing debt that will help us trim down, gaining fiscal fitness. But after we STOP the borrowing, how do we START aggressively paying off our debt? More than likely, it will take us some time to pay off our debt—in the same way it took us time to get into a financial pit hole. If you've hiked into the Grand Canyon, you know that there is a standing rule. I learned this first hand when our family backpacked to the bottom of the Canyon. Come to find out, I've been to the Canyon floor a number of times and the standing rule has never changed. Here it is: it takes twice as long to get out of the Canyon as it does to get to the bottom of the Canyon. For every hour that you descend, it takes two hours to get back up and out. Likewise, we can sign for credit in an instant, but it can take years to repay it. Let's say that a person has $4,800 charged to their credit card, and they are paying 17% interest on that card. Making minimum payments, it will take forty years to repay the balance, with $11,000 being paid in interest on the $4,800.[20]

Here's one thing to keep in mind about credit cards. We can use them to our benefit. Many credit cards come with an incentive feature, such as earning air miles that can be redeemed. If we use credit cards during the month, we must immediately set aside the money that we charged on the account, so that we can pay the entire balance due at the end of the month. Doing this, we can earn free air miles, a cash rebate, credit towards a cruise, or other incentives. Also, by having a credit card, particularly when we travel, we have access to funds in the event of an emergency. Over the years, Leah and I have paid everything possible with our credit card, and while doing so, we have earned many air miles without paying a penny of interest. For example, we earned so many air miles with credit card purchases that I was able to fly our entire family to Hawaii for our twenty-fifth wedding anniversary—and we even flew first-class. The tickets cost us nothing.

Just as Leah and I established a few spending rules by which to live, we also established a schedule to pay off our debt. Make a list of the balances you have—from least to greatest (if you have troubled accounts, you will have to give them special attention). At the head of your list, you may have a few credit card balances, followed by a student loan or home equity line balance, followed by your mortgage balance as the largest. Once you've stopped increasing your debt, begin to decrease your debt by paying off the smallest—and easiest—bal-ances. Then, celebrate! If necessary, destroy those extra credit cards. Create some momentum in the right direction. Once you've paid off the smaller debts, re-direct those payments to the next largest debt. Repay that account and celebrate. Repeat the process. As long as you are determined to practice rules for careful spending and discontinuing debt, you will have available dollars to intentionally decrease debt more quickly.

When it comes to your mortgage, there is a way to decrease it more quick-ly and painlessly. It has to do with a schedule. Scheduled mortgage payments are called the amortization. An amortization schedule will list each monthly payment and reflect the amount of principal and interest charged in that specific month's payment. Leah and I practiced this with our mortgage debt and paid off our mort-gage many years ago. Keep in mind that we do not live in a new custom-built home. We could, but we choose not to. Actually, a number of years ago, a cus-tom home builder offered to build us a large home at a greatly reduced price. We thanked him for the offer, but politely declined. Why? We asked ourselves (re-member rule #1), "Do we need this or want this?" The answer was obvious. It was not a need. We learned to be content with what we have, which includes our 2,400 square foot home that was built in 1959. A more modest purchase enabled us to borrow far less on our mortgage, which enabled us to pay it off long ago.

Here's what you do to accelerate payment on your mortgage. You print the amortization for your mortgage. Perhaps you already have it from your lend-er. When you make the current month's payment, you also include next month's *principal* along with this month's check. When you do this consistently—month by month over the life of the loan—you cut the term of your mortgage in half. A thirty-year mortgage becomes a fifteen-year mortgage. A fifteen-year mortgage becomes a seven-and-a-half-year mortgage. In the early life of a mortgage, the extra principal payments are incredibly small amounts in proportion to the interest portion of the payment. Instead of spending your income tax refund (assuming you receive one), consider using a portion of it to pay many months of extra principal on your mortgage. You will not find this difficult to do financially.

When I was a loan officer in the bank, I wrote car loans for a maximum of thirty-six months—not because I was mean-spirited, but because it was the norm. Imagine the longest length for a new car loan being three years. But in the late 70s, that quickly changed when car loans were made for four, five, and then six years. It was unheard of because a car could have little or no value by the time it was finally paid off. You and I need to understand something about debt. The length of a loan was first patterned after Scripture.

Deuteronomy 15:1-2

At the end of every seven years you must cancel debts. This is how it is to be done: Every creditor shall cancel the loan they have made to a fellow Israelite. They shall not require payment from anyone among their own people, because the Lord's time for canceling debts has been proclaimed.

From the early days of Israel, God wanted debt to be short-term—cancelling all debts every seven years. That term was used as a basis for loans in America. In the 1920s, the majority of homes were built with cash. If they did have a mortgage, it was often based on a seven year amortization. At present, the majority of homes are built with a mortgage, and the standard mortgage in America is for thirty years. Get this. Since 1995, a person in Japan can get a 100-year mortgage term! The Bible doesn't prohibit borrowing, but it certainly doesn't encourage it, either. Debt is not sinful, but it needs to be short-term. Schedule your mortgage to be repaid in half the time by including next month's principal with this month's payment. Organize the repayment of your other debts by putting them on a repayment schedule, to be deliberately paid off before their due dates. Desire to be free of debt. Get on the right side of interest – earn it, don't pay it.

WHEN SOMEONE ASKS YOU TO CO-SIGN A LOAN

There will probably come a time in life when we are asked to co-sign a loan or we want someone to co-sign a loan for us. When that moment comes, slow down and think. Think biblically. Scripture has some strong counsel on this issue.

Proverbs 11:15

"Whoever puts up security for a stranger will surely suffer, but whoever refuses to shake hands in pledge is safe."

Proverbs 17:18

"One who has no sense shakes hands in pledge and puts up security for a neighbor."

The advice is solid. Don't co-sign a loan for another person. When I was a loan officer, the bank required a co-signer if the person borrowing could not afford the loan, had little or no collateral to protect the loan, or was a credit risk. So, if we need a co-signer in order to get a loan, we should think twice about getting the loan. Clearly, we don't qualify for a loan in our own name. In this case, we should not move forward and sign on the dotted line. Likewise, if we are asked to co-sign a loan for someone, we are not helping that individual. We're actually hurting that person financially. He or she may not have the resources to service the debt, and this obligation will only further impair his or her fiscal health. Moreover, if we end up paying the debt, we will do severe damage to the relationship; resentment may last for years longer than the debt. With all that being said, let me share with you the rare moment when we can—and should—co-sign a loan. It happens when we are helping our children establish their credit rating. When I was a freshman in college, my dad co-signed a loan for me to buy my first car. It was a used Chevy Camaro and the loan was for 12 months, short in term but long enough to establish a credit rating when I was 19 years old.

Rather than co-sign for a loan for someone, consider *giving* to that someone. Jesus said, "…if you lend to those from whom you expect repayment, what credit is that to you? Even 'sinners' lend to 'sinners,' expecting to be repaid in full" (Luke 6:34). Christians in the early Church gave to those in need, and we can do the same. When we have more food or clothing than we need, it is meant to be shared. When we have more house than we can possibly live in, it can be shared. The same is true of our money. When we have more than we possibly need, it should be shared. After all, Jesus said that it is more blessed to give than to receive (Acts 20:35).

TEACHING CHILDREN ABOUT DEBT

All too often, the first experience children have with debt is when they obtain student loans for their college expenses. As well, easy credit is available to young adults through any number of credit card companies. The result? Many young adults become overextended with debt. When they graduate from college, owing tens of thousands of dollars in student loans, they find it difficult—if not impossible—to buy a car on credit, lease an apartment, and transition into independent adulthood. Other than to help them financially, is there a way to prepare them practically? Yes.

While children are growing up, consider serving as the "Bank of Mom and Dad." When your ten-year-old wants a new mountain bike or gaming system, have him buy it on credit. In order to qualify for the loan, he has to have an income to service the debt. So, hire your son to serve on your "staff." Create a time card that lists different household chores. Each day, when he completes a task, have him initial the time card next to the chore, and at the end of the week, have him turn in his time card to you, his supervisor, so that you can issue his paycheck. If he doesn't complete his chores or submit his time card, he doesn't receive a paycheck. If his behavior doesn't improve, lay him off. Seriously. It would be better for children to learn the consequences of a poor work ethic from you at home rather than in the real, grown-up world.

Once he starts earning sufficient income, he can then apply for his loan. Have him complete a simple application for the loan from you. To qualify for his loan, remember to require a down payment of twenty percent. By having to earn money for his down payment, your son learns delayed gratification, and that he must have skin in the game. Once his down payment is saved up, have him sign a loan document which clearly states when his payments are due and in what amount. Advance him the funds to make his purchase. Emphasize to your son that he needs to remain employed on your staff, earning his allowance, so that he can make his payments in a timely manner. Should he fall behind, send him a past due notice. Print it and put it on his pillow or dinner plate. If he fails to read and respond to it by engaging you—his banker—in conversation, send him a re-possession notice. If he fails to correct his past due status and continues to be non-communicative, repossess his mountain bike or gaming system. Forbid him to use it until his loan is brought current. Is this cruel and unusual punishment? No. It is responsible and practical parenting. It is essential to teach our children about work and debt while they are young. Better yet, teach them by being a good example. Have a strong work ethic coupled with responsibly managing debt. If we fail to do so, they may have to learn these lessons the hard way.

THE BIGGER PICTURE

We need to realize that when we are in debt, we experience a form of bondage. The Word states: "The rich rule over the poor, and the borrower is ser-vant to the lender" (Proverbs 22:7). The word "servant" in this verse is identical to the word used in the Old Testament to describe the Israelites while they were slaves in Egypt. When we increase our debt, we decrease our freedom. We be-come "servants to the lender." When we sign on the dotted line, we become the "servant to the lender," shackling ourselves to the bondage of debt. God did not intend for us to live in bondage. It's not in His nature.

Think with me. God sent His Son to pay our sin debt with His death on the cross. Nearing His death, Jesus declared, "It is finished," meaning that Jesus paid in full the debt of our sin. Years ago, I remember singing a chorus that declares, "He paid a debt He did not owe, I owed a debt I could not pay. I needed someone to wash my sins away. And now I sing a brand new song, 'Amazing Grace.' Christ Jesus paid a debt that I could never pay." Jesus Christ freed us from the bondage of our sin. God wants us to know freedom, even freedom from the bondage of debt.

What if we live counter-culturally? What if we swim against the current? What if we stopped looking like ducks? What if we were servants to one another, instead of being servants to the lenders? The Apostle Paul wrote: "Let no debt remain outstanding, except the continuing debt to love one another, for whoever loves others has fulfilled the law" (Romans 13:8). If we deliberately pay off our debt and pay cash as we go along, we can love others—showing them Christ-like compassion. What if we embraced debt-free living as our new normal? Imagine what we could do once we are free of paralyzing debt. We could pay our continuing debt to love one another by….

- Buying groceries for a single mom
- Helping a struggling widow with her utilities
- Rescuing someone from human-trafficking
- Taking a short-term mission trip every year
- Spontaneously helping family, friends, and strangers in need
- Providing monthly support for children in developing nations
- Adopting a child who has little hope of having a family
- Assisting our children and grandchildren when they need help early on in life
- Helping someone just released from prison get a new start in life
- Buying clothing, food, and school supplies for at-risk children
- Assisting someone entering vocational ministry on the mission field
- Helping plant a church that will reach people who are not yet Christ-followers
- Buying books or paying tuition for a person preparing to enter the ministry
- The list is endless…

Dream big.
What is possible with debt-free living?
Write your ideas here. ⟶

We feel much better when we trim down and lose a few pounds. We have more energy. We sleep better. Our strength improves. Our mental focus is clearer. The same things happen when we shed excess debt. Not only does our fiscal health improve, but our physical, mental, emotional, and even spiritual health improves dramatically.

No more Duck Syndrome. It's time to trim down.

SKIN IN THE GAME

▲ Do some brainstorming. How can you free up money to redirect toward paying off debt? Brown-bagging lunch vs. lunch out? Clipping coupons? Garage sale proceeds? A part-time job? Make a list and get moving.

▲ Make a list of your debts and determine a pay-off schedule. Plan a party and celebrate the first debt repaid!

▲ Too many credit cards? Decide which one(s) have to go. Pay off the remaining balance(s). Close the account(s) and destroy the cards.

▲ Do you have a mortgage? Print the amortization schedule. Start paying next month's principal with each month's payment. Do everything you can to pay your mortgage principal in advance.

Chapter 8
The Practice of Saving

"The wise store up choice food and olive oil,

but fools gulp theirs down."

Proverbs 21:20

Who wants to be a millionaire? It's more than a question. It's the name of a television gameshow. Originally hosted by Regis Philbin, *Who Wants to be a Millionaire* began airing on ABC in 1999. It was the first television gameshow to offer one million dollars as the top prize, and it quickly became one of the top-rated gameshows in American television history.

From gameshows to sweepstakes to lotteries, people want to become millionaires. Books abound with get-rich-quick schemes. Casinos are filled with people wanting overnight wealth. Yet most people don't realize that becoming a millionaire is within their reach. All they have to do is save their money. Think with me. If a young adult starts saving $3,500 a year and earns a return on investment (ROI) of seven percent, he or she will save over one million dollars by the time of retirement! Just start early, stick with it, and stay out of it—allow compounding interest to make a million dollars for you. And if $3,500 sounds like an impossible amount to save every year, consider that it can be done by saving $9.59—*a day!* Is it possible for us to save $10 a day, every day? We don't need to win a gameshow or have a winning lottery ticket when all we need is the desire and discipline to save.

A CULTURAL REALITY

Why do Americans rely on get-rich-quick schemes to have a financial windfall? Why do millions of Americans have nothing in savings? The answer is simple—it is not in our nature to save. In our culture, too many people live beyond their means, living paycheck to paycheck, spending more than they earn. Saving is not a priority. Spending is. People consume when they should conserve.

Since the Great Recession of 2008, most Americans live paycheck to paycheck. Gone are the savings accounts of millions of Americans, especially among the middle class. Roughly one out of three U.S. households earning $75,000 annually indicate that they are struggling financially. A survey by SunTrust and conducted by Harris Poll indicated that one in four households earning $100,000 are living paycheck to paycheck. When asked why, many respondents indicated that they are overspending, making lifestyle purchases that exceed their income. The same survey indicated that millennials are given to self-indulgence with seventy percent spending beyond their means. In a January, 2015, study by The Pew Charitable Trusts, seven out of ten Americans are struggling with too much debt and too much spending. Pew discovered that record numbers of Americans are failing to save. The bottom twenty percent of American households have only nine days of savings on hand, and the top earners have roughly fifty-two days of liquid funds available in the event of an emergency. That is far below the recommended three to six months of equivalent salary in savings.[21]

This behavior is not new to our generation. It is as old as Scripture. Jesus told a parable about a young man known as the prodigal son (Luke 15:11-20). The main point of this story is about God's forgiveness, but there's still more to the story.

In verses 11-13, three key words come to mind: immediate, immature, and immoral. The young man wanted his inheritance immediately. It was as if he were saying to his father, "Dad, I wish you were dead!" His demand for his inheritance was disrespectful, and it required his dad sell some of his life holdings in order to provide the money to his immature son. Wanting immediate gratification, he thumbed his nose at his dad, packed up all his belongings, and put some distance between the two of them as he set off for a far-away land. Once there, he wasted his inheritance in wild, immoral living. The word prodigal describes him well, as it means "wasteful, reckless."

In verses 14-19, the young man ran out of money and he then ran into a crisis—a famine. He had no food and no money with which to buy food. So, he hired himself out to work as a farm hand. On the farm, he became so hungry that he ate the very food he fed to the pigs. Remember, this young man was a Jewish boy, and Jews were required to have no contact with pigs. Ultimately, this immature son was broken—broken financially, broken emotionally with his earthly father, and broken spiritually with his heavenly Father. What crushed him? He chose to consume all that he had. He lived beyond his means.

Like the prodigal, when we live beyond our means, we demonstrate that we are immature. Think of it this way. Do you remember playing "pretend" while growing up? Girls played dress up, pretending to be moms. A bunch of us boys played army, pretending to be soldiers. We pretended to be someone we weren't. Guess what? We're still playing the pretend game when we live beyond our means. The word "pretend" means to make believe, to deceive. When we live beyond our means, we are pretending to be someone we're not. We're living a lie. Also, like the prodigal, people living beyond their means live for the moment, wanting immediate gratification. It's no wonder people are financially broke.

We need to be more like another young guy, whose name was Joseph. His story is told in Genesis 37-50. He was sold into slavery at the age of seventeen by his older brothers; and though he was an innocent man, he ended up in prison. While Joseph was serving his sentence, the Pharaoh of Egypt had two dreams that deeply troubled him. He wanted the dreams interpreted, but no one in the royal court could do so. Eventually, Pharaoh learned that Joseph had the ability to interpret dreams. Summoned to the palace, Joseph was cleaned up and brought before Egypt's king.

Joseph told Pharaoh that his two dreams were one and the same. First, Egypt would experience seven years of agricultural bounty, enjoying vast and abundant harvests. Following the record years of plenty, there would be seven consecutive years of famine, the likes of which Egypt had never before experienced. Pharaoh was stunned by the interpretation, and he rewarded Joseph by naming him "Vice-President" of Egypt. Joseph went from prisoner to prince.

Joseph was charged with the responsibility of taking Egypt through the next fourteen years. He organized the planting of crops, managed the building of storehouses, developed the accounting methods for distributing grain, and more. The plan was for Egypt's farmers to give Joseph twenty percent of their record harvests, only to later buy back the grain during record famine. Now think with me. What if Joseph had allowed the people to consume all of the grain during the seven years of plenty? Such conspicuous consumption would have resulted in massive death. Joseph saved the lives of untold numbers of people because he saved the grain. Joseph was wise beyond his years, for: "The wise store up choice food and olive oil, but fools gulp theirs down" (Proverbs 21:20).

If we hope to be financially healthy, we have to save. We can't consume everything we earn. We can't be wasteful and reckless when it comes to our money and the things that money can buy. We need to set money aside because we are going to need it. Emergencies happen. Unexpected expenses occur. Downturns in the economy are certain. If you were to lose your job, do you have three to six months of income in a savings account? If the transmission were to go out on your car, do you have a few thousand dollars in savings for the repair? If your child became seriously ill and you incurred high medical expenses as a result, do you have money to pay the deductible? We must have money in savings for sudden expenses in the present, as well as for those looming expenses of tomorrow: braces for the children, college tuition, our eventual retirement, and more.

Job security is not the same as it was a generation ago. As mentioned earlier, my dad had one employer his entire life, which is now rare. Today, an individual spends 4.4 years at a job before moving along to another, and by retiring, will have ten to twelve different jobs. Knowing that job security is a thing of the past, how can we afford not to have some savings to sustain us between jobs? And what if we hate our job? Do we stay or do we look for new work? In his memoir, Andre Agassi said, "I hate tennis. I hate it with a dark, secret passion and always have...I hate tennis, hate it with all my heart, and still I keep playing, keep hitting all morning and all afternoon, because I have no choice."[22] After winning eight grand slam tournaments, along with millions of dollars, the former number one ranked tennis player in the world hated his work—and felt trapped by it. What about us? If we had some money saved, there's a better chance we could give notice to our employer and look for another job. Don't consume every dollar. Conserve some of those dollars. Here's how.

SKIN IN THE GAME

▲ With whom do you identify more: the prodigal son or Joseph? Why? What behaviors or attitudes in your life make you appear more like the one and less like the other? Be specific.

▲ Do you have savings for emergencies and unexpected life circumstances? If not, why not? If so, how careful are you to not spend this money?

AN INDIVIDUAL NECESSITY

Capital One Bank did a survey of two thousand adults, asking the question: "Why do we save?" Many respondents indicated that they save in order to pay off debt and to provide for retirement. Yet, fifteen percent of those polled said saving is the right thing to do.[23] Imagine that. There are people out there who still know that they should save, because it is right and good. I hope we are numbered among them. We need to save.

In elementary school, we were taught the interrogatives of speech: who, what, when, where, why, and how. These questions are rightly named because, when asked, they serve to interrogate a situation. These fundamental questions unlock information about the issue at hand. So, using the interrogatives of speech, let's understand more clearly the practice of saving.

WHAT is saving?

Saving is the practice of intentionally setting aside a portion of what we have for the "tomorrows" of life, as stated in Proverbs 21:20. Scripture was written in the context of an agriculturally-based economy. Wealth was held in commodities, such as in livestock and crops. So, this verse indicates that the wise person doesn't consume all of his crops, but sets some aside for the future, even for bartering with other individuals. In our culture, wealth is primarily held in the form of money, and we are well-advised to deliberately set aside a portion of what we earn or are given.

WHO should save?

Everyone. Young and old, alike, should save. Get pre-school children a piggy-bank and teach them to put coins into it. When they grow up a little more, open a savings account at the bank with them. The sooner we teach our children about saving, the better. And once we start saving, at whatever age that happens, don't stop. Even those who are retired should continue to save.

HOW much should we save?

This varies among people, but there are some typical amounts that help us start saving, such as the 10-10-80 rule (which can be taught to children and teens). When you receive a paycheck, give 10% of it away (i.e., tithe—see Chapter 10 The Practice of Giving). Then, save 10% of that paycheck, using 80% for other expenses. Another way to answer this question is to consider your monthly income. It is a standard practice to have three to six months of income set aside in the event of an emergency. This money is often called contingency funds, and such savings are not to be used except for an emergency. Still another way to answer this question is to save a percentage of the value of your home. It is a rule of thumb to save 3% of the market value of your home for repairs and maintenance. If a person's home has a market value of $150,000, they would save $4,500 a year for the purpose of replacing the furnace and air-conditioner, redecorating the family room, etc. Allowing this amount of money to accumulate would enable the homeowner to pay cash for a kitchen or bathroom remodeling project.

WHEN should we start saving?

Immediately. Time is of the essence. The earlier a person begins to save, the better. Teaching children this discipline is essential if they want to have money to buy a car in the future, have a down payment on their first home, or have tuition money for college. Once we start saving, we should stick with it, and stay out of it! When I was in graduate school (the first time around), I enrolled full time. It was my hope to finish seminary as quickly as possible and to be ordained into the ministry. While in seminary, I worked twenty hours a week as a bank teller, earning $4.25 an hour, which was minimum wage at the time. My gross paycheck each week was $80, and there were three of us living off that income—Leah, myself, and our one-year-old son. Still, I opened an IRA (Individual Retirement Account) and deposited $25 a month into that account. I was twenty-four years old at the time. We started saving for retirement when we were young. We have stayed with it, generously adding to our retirement investments. And, we have stayed out of them. With retirement on our horizon, we are grateful we did so. Moreover, by starting to save early, and staying out of the savings, the power of compounding interest has worked to our advantage. Compounding interest happens when interest is paid on the savings balance *plus* paid on the interest it has already earned. We earn interest on our interest. Get rid of debt as quickly as possible. Stop paying interest. Start saving as soon as possible, and you will get on the *right side* of interest.

To understand the importance of starting early and staying out of it when it comes to saving, we need to be familiar with the Rule of 72, which determines how long it will take for our savings to double. The rule is simply this: divide 72 by your interest rate. For example, Leah and I have some certificates of deposit that currently earn 5% interest, and when I divide 72 by 5, it will take us 15 years for that account to double—assuming we keep the 5% rate—and we stay out of those accounts. Just remember to start saving early, stick with it, and stay out of it.

WHERE should we save?

Not in a mattress. In Israel, an elderly woman put her entire life savings into her mattress for safe keeping. Night after night, she slept on one million dollars in American and Israeli currency, and knowing that her entire life savings was well within her reach, she slept well. Why put such an enormous amount of money in a mattress? This elderly woman had lived through many economic downturns, and she had lost trust in the banking system. Actually, the woman was of the opinion you could not trust anyone with your savings. Not even her daughter knew of her stash of cash. This is where this story takes a turn—one for the worse. When the daughter noticed how lumpy her aged mother's mattress was, she decided to surprise her by buying her a new mattress. While her mother was away, the daughter had the new mattress delivered and the old mattress taken away to the garbage. The daughter wanted her mother to be surprised when she slipped into bed that first night and felt the soft, comfortable mattress. That did not happen. Lying on her bed, the elderly woman recognized the new feel of the mattress, and she literally screamed! When this story was told on the news, a video clip showed the daughter digging through a dump, looking for the missing mattress—and one million dollars![24]

There are far better places in which to save our money than in mattresses. Not ranked in any particular order, here are some places where you can put your savings.

Passbook Savings Account	Money Market Checking Account
Certificates of Deposit	U.S. Savings Bonds
Mutual Funds	U.S. Treasury Securities
Stocks & Bonds	529 Educational Savings Accounts
Real Estate	Precious Metals (gold/silver/platinum)
Whole Life Insurance	Life Insurance Annuities
Collectibles (antiques, etc.)	Investment in a Business

Keep in mind that some savings vehicles carry greater risk than others. A rule of thumb to remember is that the lower the risk of the investment, the lower the rate of return. Since banks carry FDIC protection and your savings vehicle at the bank is insured against loss, your rate of return will be low. On the other hand, if you are willing to invest in stocks, you can have much higher yields, but with a much greater risk of losing part or all of your investment. This is an important issue. The older we are, the less risk we should take. Why? With retirement in the near future, we have fewer years to recapture any lost funds from a failed investment. On the flipside, the younger you are, the greater risk you can take because you will have more time to recover financially should you experience a loss of your investment. For all ages, one way to protect your savings is by diversifying. "Don't put all of your eggs in the same basket" is an old saying that packs a punch. If all of your savings are in one place, and that one place experiences an economic downturn, you can potentially lose all of your savings.

A word of warning here: beware of scams. We are living in an era of fraud. Not only do people want to steal our identity, they want to steal our money. People who are eager to get rich quickly are just as eager to scam us. It is not uncommon to hear in the news about individuals being arrested on charges of investment fraud. For many of us, we will long remember convicted felon Bernie Madoff, who "made off" with nearly sixty-five billion dollars belonging to his investors. His life-long claim to fame is having orchestrated the largest Ponzi scheme in all of modern history, absconding with the savings of literally thousands of clients, many of whom are now financially destroyed. After living life as a billionaire, Madoff will die in prison, serving a one-hundred-fifty-year prison term that he began at the age of seventy.

Therefore, beware of scams. If the deal is too good to be true, it probably is, and it may be a scam. If the individual promoting the investment opportunity offers vague answers to your questions, beware that it may be a potential scam. If you can find little or no written information about the investment, it may be a scam. If the individual contacting you is pressuring you to make an immediate investment, it could be a scam. Be skeptical of the latest fad or hot tip.

WHY should we save?

We can answer this interrogative with two simple words: care and share. We must save because we must care for ourselves and others. Scripture declares: "Anyone does not provide for their relatives, and especially for their own household, has denied the faith and is worse than an unbeliever" (1 Timothy 5:8). We need to save so that we have resources with which to care for those in our family. This value is deeply rooted in Scripture. When Jesus was hanging on the cross, He made provision for His mother's needs by telling the disciple John that he should now consider himself Mary's son. Why did Jesus do that? It was ex-pected of the eldest son to care for his elderly parents, particularly for a widowed mother, and even for unmarried sisters. In Scripture, the eldest son received a larger inheritance for just this purpose.

From his early twenties, my dad cared for his widowed mom. My grand-mother lived with us from the time my parents married. She was widowed at a young age, and her husband, my grandfather, had immigrated to America from Sweden. He had few resources at the time of his death, and my grandmother had only a sixth-grade education. Instead of saving up for a down payment on a home of their own, my parents saved some money to add a two-bedroom in-law quarters on to my grandmother's house in which to live. My grandmother lived in that house, being cared for by my dad, until she was eighty-seven years old. By that time she went into a nursing home, where she died a few weeks later. My parents provided care for my grandmother until they could no longer provide her an appropriate level of medical care.

As parents, if we want our children to go to college, should we really shift the entire financial cost to the government or a student loan program? It is right for us to expect our children to excel in hopes of earning scholarship funds, but do we then assume that federal or state financial aid should cover the remainder of the cost? Do we shift responsibility to our children and ask them to pay for the cost of their education by taking out tens of thousands of dollars in student loans? While our children are growing up, do we conserve our money by saving for their college educations or do we consume our money by spending it on what we want?

Not only do we save to care for others, we save because we want to share with others. In Acts 4:36-37, we are told that a man named Joseph sold a field that he owned and gave the money to the leaders of the church in Jerusalem. Though Joseph was his legal name, the disciples gave him a nickname—Barnabas, which means Son of Encouragement. The phrase "son of" is significant. It was commonly used in Bible days. For example, Jesus gave James and John, the sons of Zebedee, a nickname—Sons of Thunder (Mark 3:17). The phrase "sons of" identifies a dominant trait. In this case, James and John had volatile, aggressive temperaments. Barnabas, on the other hand, had a dominant trait of encouragement. He helped people, so much so, that he did not keep a piece of real estate for himself. Though the field was a source of savings for him, he willingly shared with the church. Similarly, we save so that we can share with others. Rather than spend every dollar on ourselves, we set aside some of the earnings and money we receive (i.e., inheritance, tax refunds, etc.) to share with individuals in need, to share with charitable organizations, etc. Caring and sharing are two biblical reasons why we save.

Leah and I have lived by a rule of thumb when it comes to why we save. That rule is this: just because we *can* doesn't mean we *should*. Just because we have money saved doesn't mean we should spend it. When I was growing up, my parents often said, "We can't afford it." While our sons were growing up, we could afford what they wanted, but we told them, "We choose not to spend money that way." There is a difference. Throughout our marriage, Leah and I pursued the biblical principles and financial practices in this book, and by God's grace, we have more than enough resources to do or buy whatever we want. Yet, just because we can doesn't mean we should. Rather than consume all of your income, try to save a portion of it so that you can *care* for and *share* with others. It's biblical.

If anyone practiced saving, Oseola McCarty did. However, to most people, Miss McCarty lived a meager and ordinary life. She had one occupation her entire life, and that was doing laundry. Oseola washed, dried, and ironed clothes for other people. When she died of cancer at the age of 91, Ms. McCarty left behind quite a legacy. She never owned a car and walked wherever she went. She pushed a shopping cart nearly a mile to get groceries. In 1947, her uncle gave her the house in which she lived until her death. Early in life, Ms. McCarty's mother taught her how to save money. With earnings from her humble, life-long occupation of doing laundry, Ms. McCarty gave the University of Southern Mississippi $150,000! Oseola McCarty lived by the teaching of Jesus, "It is more blessed to give than to receive" (see Acts 20:35). She cared for others, and in the end, she shared with others that which she had saved. Oseola lived within her means, consuming less and conserving more. Oseola McCarty learned how to live with less in this land of more.[25]

SKIN IN THE GAME

▲ What percent of your income do you save?

▲ What are you saving for? Be specific.

▲ Does the purpose for your saving have anything to do with caring or sharing with others?

▲ Calculate how many years it will take your money to double by applying the Rule of 72 to your specific savings account.

▲ Have you ever been scammed? If so, how could you have caught it before it caught you?

▲ How does the rule "just because you can doesn't mean you should" apply to your life?

Chapter 9
The Practice of Budgeting

"Now it is required that those who have been given
a trust must prove faithful."
1 Corinthians 4:2

Living in Indianapolis, I've been to the Indianapolis 500 a few times. Once you attend, you know that the motto is true, as it is the "greatest spectacle in racing." One of the fascinating features of the race happens in the pit, and not on the course. Back in the 1950s, the pit crew consisted of four men, including the driver. In just one minute, the four-man crew replaced two tires and filled the tank with gas. Today's pit crew looks and acts much differently. It has eleven members on the team, and if you watch them closely, six have direct contact with the car—changing tires and refueling in less than eight seconds—while five people serve behind the wall. The team works together. They have a plan and every person does his part to make the plan work.

We now come to a practice in financial health that involves a plan, and every person in the family has to help if the plan is to work—particularly mom and dad. When God gives to us a marriage and family, He has given to us a trust. The Word tells us that when we're given a trust, we must be faithful to fulfill that trust. We must care for those relationships in every dimension, including financially. One of the tools to help us achieve financial health is the practice of budgeting, and each person in the family must do his or her part if it is to work. Budgeting is not a practice just for those who are married with children. It is also essential for those who are single; whether yet to be married, divorced, or widowed.

THE PROBLEM

Yet, there is a problem. Not everyone wants to live by a budget. Peter Dunn, a financial planner, writes: "People hate budgeting. They just do. It's kinda like people hate exercising. But that doesn't mean you shouldn't do both. It's no surprise those people who hate exercising and budgeting the most are often the people who need to exercise and budget the most."[26]

Increasing numbers of people do not live by a budget because they do not have a budget. A family budget identifies income and expenses, enabling a family to live within its income. When a family or individual does not have a spending plan, people take a financial risk. An old and familiar saying reflects this reality: "To fail to plan is to plan to fail."

People used to monitor their spending by using their checking accounts. It was a common practice for people to actually balance their checking accounts every month when the statement arrived in the mail. Those days are gone. Just ask people if they balance their checking accounts, and they often answer, "No." In the last decade, debit cards have outpaced the writing of checks. It is far easier to swipe a debit card than it is to write a check or even to pay cash. It is easy to spend money using a debit card, and when people casually swipe the card, their spending can easily exceed their income. Combine this habit with the practice of not balancing a checking account every month, and you have a higher chance of living in a state of financial fog.

This problem is common in America, but not in Germany. Think back with me. Germany was devastated financially in World War II. Not only did they lose the war, they lost much more. Cities were destroyed in Allied bombing raids. Business infra-structure was shattered. Government—at every level—was obliterated. The German people were decimated. In response, they were determined to re-build both their country and their culture. Eventually, their economy became inter-nationally known and respected as their currency , the deutschmark, emerged as a symbol of German pride.   When the European Union was formed, the deutsch-mark gave way to the euro. Germany responded by insisting that a 500 euro bill be created in the new currency system because Germans were accustomed to pay-ing cash for many of their expenses. In 2014, the Central Bank of Germany did a study indicating that eighty percent of their financial transactions are done in cash. The German culture prides itself on honoring its obligations, being economically frugal, and avoiding debt. Many Germans frown on the use of credit cards. After all, *schuld*, the German word for debt, means guilt. Karl Brenke, an analyst at the German Economic Institute, said, "People want to be in complete control over their spending. The logic is that when you pay in cash you can only pay as much mon-ey as you have available, so you won't overspend." Similarly, Berlin stonemason, Sebastian Savelsberg, said, "Of course I prefer paying cash. I have a much better overview of my finances that way."[27]

Germany did not continue to live in its past, but the people certainly learned from it. Can we say the same? In the 1930s, America experienced the Great Depression. Those who lived through it learned from their past. My parents were teenagers then, and the Depression impacted how they lived financially. Ev-ery Saturday morning, I watched my dad as he sat at the kitchen table, paying his bills—and he did so with cash. My dad would put cash into envelopes for utility companies and more, and then drive them to the neighborhood hardware store, where he bought money orders for each of the bills. His entire life, he never had a checking account. Though he kept some money in the bank, he—along with many others who went through the Depression—did not trust the banking system. It was a common practice for my dad to cash his pay check and then hide a sizeable amount of cash in the house. My folks not only paid cash for everything, but they saved and lived within a budget. Their generation learned from the past, and it's time for our generation to do the same.

Let's take a lesson for life today from long ago in the past. In Luke 14:28-30, Jesus described what it cost to follow Him as a disciple. He used an analogy and said, "Suppose one of you wants to build a tower. Will he not first sit down and estimate the cost to see if he has enough money to complete it? For if he lays the foundation and is not able to finish it, everyone who sees it will ridicule him, saying, 'This fellow began to build and was unable to finish.'" The lesson we are to learn here—from the long ago past—is to count the cost. This lesson applies to many dimensions of life, even that of our personal finances. If we are building a house or remodeling the kitchen, count the cost of the project by developing a budget. If we are selecting a college to attend or a car to purchase, count the cost by comparing prices and benefits. Another way of saying count the cost is practice budgeting.

Proverbs 27:23-24 states, "Be sure you know the condition of your flocks, give careful attention to your herds; for riches do not endure forever and a crown is not secure for all generations." Remember, the Bible was written in an agricultural age. Wealth was held in livestock and crops. The phrase "know the condition of your flocks, give careful attention to your herds" means that we are to know the condition of our bank accounts, our different assets, our property, our debt, and more. We must know every aspect of our finances, and the practice of budgeting allows us to do just that.

SKIN IN THE GAME

> ▲ Do you balance your checking account regularly? If so, what do you learn about your spending pattern? If not, why not?
>
> ▲ Describe the "condition of your flocks" (i.e., your finances). Be specific. What is your debt load? How much money do you have invested? Are you sufficiently insured?
>
> ▲ What is your attitude about budgeting? Does it need to change? If so, how and why?

THE PLAN

Budgeting is planning, and there are examples of planning throughout the Scriptures. In the Old Testament, Joseph was an expert at planning. Remember in Chapter 9 we talked about how he planned to harvest the largest crops during seven years of plenty in ancient Egypt. He then planned how to disburse the grain equitably during the seven years of record famine (Genesis 37-50). There was also Nehemiah who the Lord stirred to rebuild the walls around Jerusalem, which had been destroyed by the armies of King Nebuchadnezzar of Babylon. Once Nehemiah arrived in Jerusalem, he examined the debris field. Interestingly, he did this at night so as not to be distracted by people. Nehemiah needed time to think, to formulate a plan for the rebuilding of the walls and the placement of the gates as quickly as possible (Nehemiah 2:11-18).

In the New Testament, we read of how the early church in Jerusalem had a food crisis. The Greek-speaking widows among them were being overlooked in the daily distribution of food. The widows went to bed hungry night after night. The disciples came up with a plan, and once in place, the widows were well-fed and the church in Jerusalem continued to grow. Jesus Christ had a plan for winning the world to Himself. He told His followers to go and make disciples of all nations (i.e., people groups) by baptizing them into the Father, Son, and Holy Spirit, teaching them to obey all of His commandments (Matthew 28:18-20). Christians are to reach others and then teach others. Jesus provided more details to His plan when He told His disciples that they were to wait for the power of the Holy Spirit to come on them. Then they would be empowered to be His witnesses, beginning in Jerusalem, then going to Judea, then into Samaria, and finally to the ends of the earth (Acts 1:8). The Bible is full of examples of people who took seriously the practice of planning. We should follow their example.

Planning is the result of analytical thinking. Psalm 139 states that we are fearfully and wonderfully made (vs. 14). Our minds are a gift from God, therefore we should use them. One of my favorite verses related to analytical thinking is 1 Chronicles 12:32, that from Issachar, there were men who understood the times and knew what Israel should do. They were able to read their culture and respond appropriately. In the same way, we must use our minds to think analytically about our finances, and to respond appropriately. Let's now use our minds to explore what it means to practice budgeting.

The Numerical Side of a Budget

Obviously, budgeting involves numbers, and is nothing more than an intentional plan for the spending of your money. If you have never taken time to create such a plan, do so now. This will not be a waste of time and effort, nor will it be unnecessarily difficult. Keep this as simple as possible so that it will be useful to you. You can do this with pen and paper (you had better start with pencil so that you can erase), or you can do this digitally, using an excel spreadsheet or mobile app. Making a spending plan is an essential practice if we are to have healthy finances.

If you are married, be sure to involve your spouse in this process. Nothing can derail this more quickly than for a husband and a wife to have completely different perspectives regarding their spending plan. Before beginning, have a conversation about your financial goals. Identify your goals as either immediate, intermediate, or long term. An immediate goal could be to save money for Christmas presents whereas an intermediate goal could be paying off a credit card, and a long term goal might be to pay off student loans or even the home mortgage. The point is: make a plan. Again, if we fail to plan, we plan to fail. Now let's review some simple, necessary steps when it comes to building a budget.

Step One: List All Sources of Income

It is important to identify the source and frequency of your income, such as: paychecks, work bonuses, sales commissions, interest on investments, rental income, monetary gifts, stock dividends, tax refunds, proceeds from sales, etc. It is important to identify how often you receive this income. Are you paid once a week, twice a month, once a month, etc.? Is your income strictly commissions from sales? Don't forget it's important to list the gross amount of earnings on your budget worksheet. Once you have listed your income and its frequency, you are ready for the next step.

Step Two: List All Expenses

List each of your expenses. You may want to group them together in categories, such as those related to your car, your home, your insurances, your health, etc. Look through your check book or your online banking statements and review your spending. Be as thorough as possible in compiling this list.

AUTO EXPENSES:
Car Payment
Gasoline
Maintenance
Insurance

HOUSING EXPENSES:
House payment/rent
Utilities (Cable, electric, phone, gas, water, etc.)
Property Taxes
Insurance (home owners/renter's)
Repairs & Maintenance
Furnishings

HEALTH CARE:
Eye
Dental
Medical

OTHER:
Cell Phone
Clothing
Credit Cards
Debt (Other than car/mortgage)
Food
Income Taxes

Insurances (Life, health, disability, etc.)

Personal Expenses (Hair care, etc.)

Recreation (dinner out, travel, etc.)

Savings (Emergency, college, retirement, etc.)

School Expenses (books, athletics, uniforms, supplies, etc.)

Tithes

Miscellaneous

Once you have completed the list, identify those expenses that are fixed and recurring. Enter the dollar amount next to these expenses. For all others, enter an amount based on previous spending or a future spending estimate. If you have never built a personal budget or don't have a clue how much to safely spend in these categories, here are some standard percentages of income provided by Dave Ramsey, author of *The Total Money Makeover: A Proven Plan for Financial Fitness* (Nelson Books, 2013). Ramsey recommends the following: charitable giving 10—15%; savings 5-10%; housing 25-35%; utilities 5-10%; transportation 10-15%; food 5-15%; clothing 2-7%; medical/health 5-10%; personal 5-10%; recreation 5-10%; and debt 5-10%. Many factors will impact the percentage you spend on particular expenses. It may be that you have a large family with growing children, or you may live in a place with an exceptionally high cost of living. These percentages are helpful guidelines, not restrictive straightjackets.

Step Three: Calculate the Difference & Make Adjustments

Calculate your total income and your total expenses. Hopefully, your income will exceed your expenses. If so, consider what to do with your excess income. In light of your immediate, intermediate, and long-term financial goals, how can you best use this unspent income? Could you pay off a credit card or student loan? Could this be used towards a down payment on a home or used to start an emergency savings account? Do not spend the excess haphazardly.

If your expenses exceed your income, you will need to adjust your spending. To do so, examine which categories are significantly beyond the suggested percentage guideline. You will have to reduce spending in one or more categories in order to balance your budget. Failure to do so will result in living paycheck to paycheck, and it will actually create a spending deficit. The longer you keep spending more money than you make, the longer it will take for you to recover financially.

Step Four: Make Budgeting a Regular Practice

Once you create a budget, use it. When you get paid, run the budget and stay within the guidelines you have set. The easiest way to make this happen is to put all of your income into your checking account, which should be interest-bearing. Most banking institutions compete with one another for your business by offering checking accounts that pay a nominal amount of interest. Deposit all of your income into this account and pay all of your expenses out of this account so that you can track your spending. If this sounds complicated to you, make it simple by using the "envelope system." Make an envelope for every expense you have (i.e., rent/house payment, gas, car payment, groceries, tithe, etc.). Write the dollar amount of that expense on that envelope. Then, cash your paycheck and put the amount of money needed for that expense into the envelope. Don't take any money out of the envelopes! Save it up from pay period to pay period, and you will have sufficient money on hand when that expense comes due.

Keep in mind that if you are paid weekly and you have a monthly mortgage payment, you must set aside money from each paycheck towards that monthly expense. Many expenses are similar, such as insurance premiums, utilities, etc. As well, when you use your credit card, be sure to set aside a sum of money in your checking account with which to pay the entire statement balance when you receive it in the mail. Refuse to pay the exorbitant interest rates charged by credit card companies. Get on the right side of interest. If you build and keep a good budget, you can use a credit card to track your spending and to earn some rewards, like that of air miles, cash-rewards, and more.

The Food and Drug Administration requires calorie labeling on menus of restaurant chains, yet it doesn't appear that the information is changing our eating habits. Studies reveal that three out of four Americans like and support calorie labeling, but it hasn't brought about any significant change in what we eat. Though we know there are fewer calories in a roasted chicken sandwich than a double cheeseburger, we continue to eat what we want to eat.[28] Similarly, even though we know that budgeting is good for us financially, it doesn't magically change our ways. Budgeting only works when we work the budget. Even at our age, Leah and I still use a budget. Every week, I crunch the numbers, just as I have done since the day we were married long ago. We never outgrow this discipline because budgeting enables us to "know the condition of our flocks" (Proverbs 27:23).

The Biblical Side of a Budget

Early in our marriage, Leah and I came to appreciate a formula for budgeting that had nothing to do with crunching numbers, but had everything to do with obeying Scripture. The insight came to us from Matthew 4:1-11, which describes Satan's temptation of Jesus. Think through the three specific temptations. First, Satan tempted Jesus to turn stones into delicious bread. Though He was famished from forty days of fasting, Jesus replied that man doesn't live by bread alone but by every word that comes from the mouth of God. Jesus was biblical. Second, Satan took Jesus to a high point of the Temple and tempted Him to jump. Jesus replied that no one should put the Lord to the test by trying to force God to come to the rescue. Jesus was sensible. Finally, Satan offered Jesus the kingdoms of the world. They could all be His if He would only bow down and worship Satan. Jesus refused because He worshipped God and served Him only. Jesus was loyal. These three words became very important to Leah and me. Biblical. Sensible. Loyal. Those are attitudes and actions on which to build a budget.

Here's an example of how this has worked out in my life. I enjoy fast, sporty cars. There was a time when I was looking at a new, fire-engine red, six-speed, convertible Corvette. I didn't need it; I wanted it. We had the money in savings, but we have this rule: "Just because we can doesn't mean we should." I was tempted to buy the car, but then the temptation account of Jesus came to mind. I asked myself three questions: *Am I being biblical?* The Bible teaches contentment (see Chapter 3), but I was not content at the time with the car I was driving. *Am I being sensible?* Driving around in a shiny, new Corvette when my sons were about to leave for college was not sensible. Actually, it would have looked insane! Why would I consume money from savings to drive a car that would turn heads when I needed to use those savings to send my sons off to college? *Am I being loyal?* By spending this money on myself, how was I being loyal to the kingdom of God? Would it hinder our ability to give tithes and offerings to God? Money is saved to care for and share with others.

This three-question formula helps us budget our money by slowing us down and keeping us from making hasty financial decisions. If we want to build a fine custom home, first ask: "Is this biblical?" Have we wrestled the issue of contentment to the ground? Are we content with the home we already have? "Is this sensible?" If we build this new custom home, does this make sense? Does the new address and home look more sensational than our current address and home? If we build the home and then lose our jobs, will God have to come to our rescue financially? "Is this loyal?" If we build our new home, will we be loyal to God by continuing to tithe, or will the new and increased house payment take from or even eliminate our ability to tithe? Be biblical. Be sensible. Be loyal. These attitudes and actions provide a strong foundation on which to practice budgeting.

Learning typically happens in three stages. Stage 1: We acquire information. As children, we learned the alphabet, shapes, colors, numbers, etc. Stage 2: We try and understand what we have learned. As adolescents, we asked the question "why" in response to the information we acquired in the first stage. Stage 3: We apply information to life. In this stage, we begin to experience wisdom, which is the application of knowledge. Like water flooding over the precipice of Niagara Falls, we are awash in a daily deluge of information—even information about our finances. As we acquire more information about budgeting, we can become wise when we apply it to our everyday lives. After all, "by wisdom a house is built, and through understanding it is established" (Proverbs 24:3).

SKIN IN THE GAME

▲ Does your income exceed your expenses, or do your expenses exceed your income?

▲ Depending on your answer the question above, how are you responding to your current financial condition?

▲ What are your immediate, intermediate, and long-term financial goals? If you don't have specific financial goals, why not?

Chapter 10
The Practice of Giving

"...the Lord Jesus Himself said,
'It is more blessed to give than to receive.'"
Acts 20:35

Hot topics swirl around us at ever-increasing speed. From immigration to religious radicalism to same-sex marriage, some topics have the power to demand our attention around the clock. In recent years one subject has topped the rest: the topic of money. A survey by Wells Fargo & Company revealed forty-four percent of Americans polled claimed that a discussion about personal finances is the most difficult conversation to have with another person.[29]   Even so, you and I know that another money-related issue can make a conversation go nuclear. It is the topic of giving, and it has potential to make any conversation explosive.

We may not want to talk about giving, but we must. It is an essential part of our financial wellbeing. Just as healthy eating and regular exercise contribute to our physical health, generous and regular giving contributes to our fiscal health. Like it or not, it is a necessary topic of conversation, and one that God wants to have with us. The Bible has more than 2,350 verses that talk about money-related issues, and many of them speak directly about giving. Come to think of it, the opening pages of Scripture introduce us to the most generous Giver of all time, and that person is God. God gave us an indescribable universe and an equally indescribable human body with which to engage His creation.

We keep pictures on our smart phones, tablets, and computers. We may even keep pictures in conventional photo albums. This should come as no surprise since "a picture speaks a thousand words." Think with me. What if we thought of the Bible as a photo album? It is full of "snapshots" that reveal something unique about the nature of God. Can you spot it in these few "pictures" below?

Genesis 1:29

Then God said, "I **give** you every seed-bearing plant on the face of the whole earth and every tree that has fruit with seed in it. They will be yours for food.

Deuteronomy 8:10

When you have eaten and are satisfied, praise the LORD your God for the good land he has **given** you.

Jeremiah 24:7

I will **give** them a heart to know me, that I am the LORD. They will be my people, and I will be their God, for they will return to me with all their heart.

Ezekiel 11:19

I will **give** them an undivided heart and put a new spirit in them; I will remove from them their heart of stone and give them a heart of flesh.

Luke 11:13

"If you, then, though you are evil, know how to give good gifts to your children, how much more will your Father in heaven **give** the Holy Spirit to those who ask him!

John 3:16

God so loved the world that He **gave** His one and only Son…

These are just a few of the many snapshots in the Bible that clearly reveal the nature of God. And what do we learn about who God is? He is inexpressibly generous, and we belong to Him. From the very beginning of measured time, God has been lavishly generous with us, and He continues to be so today. God made the first move of generosity when He breathed life into us, and in creating a universe that is beyond all human understanding. However, His crowning act of generosity was the gift of His one and only Son, Jesus Christ, so that we could have life everlasting.

Leah and I have three generations of wedding pictures in our home, and looking at them, there is a striking resemblance between my dad, myself, and my son when we were each in our early twenties. We resemble one another. This is not just true of my family. In general, family photos allow family members to see how much they resemble one another. This is also the case in God's family. So the question for us is whether or not we resemble our heavenly Father? Having been made in His image, are we generous?

THE STRUGGLE WITH GIVING

An individual or family may struggle with healthy eating and regular exercise. In the same way, individuals or families can struggle with generous and regular giving. The numbers speak for themselves. Giving across America is declining; and in particular, giving to churches is down. In his book *The Great Evangelical Recession*, pastor and author John Dickerson describes the current state of giving in the American church: "The financial crisis is not a shortage of funds. It is a shortage of commitment. We do not believe in tithing or for that matter, generous giving." He goes on to say, "More importantly, we do not believe Jesus' simple, direct statement, 'Where your treasure is, there your heart will be also' (Luke 12:34). If Jesus' claim is true, then the heart of the typical American evangelical is not in Christ's kingdom. Our hearts are in our cars, credit cards, mortgages, and retirement savings."[30]

On his long-running television show *Late Night with David Letterman,* the Hoosier native made famous his "Top Ten List," covering an expansive number of topics. Come to think of it, we can quickly create a top ten list of the excuses we use to justify not giving to God. Not in any particular order, here are some of the most popular excuses for not giving to God:

1) *We are not content with what we have.*

   We live beyond our means—spending more money than we earn by financing our conspicuous consumption.

2) *We do not live by a budget.*

   Rather than have a spending plan, we just spend; and in the end, we have nothing left to give to God.

3) *We covet and compete.*

When we see the neighbors driving a new car, we want one. When friends tell of us of their latest cruise, we want to enjoy the same. When people walk past us in designer jeans, we want a pair. Not only do we want to keep up with the Joneses, we want more than what the Joneses have. And to have more, we give less—or nothing at all.

4) *We want immediate gratification.*

Want that new coat or new kitchen? Why wait? Whether it is a night out on the town or a vacation out of town, just use credit. Credit cards are prolific. Offers for instant credit arrive weekly—if not daily—in the mail. Delaying gratification is a practice from the past, but without it, we prevent ourselves from giving to God in the present.

5) *We are mired down in debt.*

Easy credit means easy debt. Student loans, car payments, mortgages, credit card charges, home equity lines—we write checks to all of these, and yet fail to write a check to God.

6) *We delay giving.*

We rationalize that we are not in the right season of life to give. We say, "When I graduate from college, I'll give. When I get the job promotion, I'll give. When I receive the bonus or the tax refund, I'll give. When I get married, I'll give. When the kids are grown and gone, I'll give." Whatever reason we give for delaying our giving, the reason is wrong. Delayed giving is disobedience to God.

7) *We already give enough.*

When it comes time for the offering, a twenty dollar bill looks pretty big in a worship service. We think twice about putting it—or more—into the offering. Yet, if we happen to be at the gas station, the grocery store, a football game, at the movies, or elsewhere, we don't think twice about using that same twenty dollars. It doesn't look nearly that big. We excuse ourselves from giving *more* because in our thinking – we've already given enough.

8) *Money-and the things money can buy-makes us feel safe.*

Some people feel secure when they are surrounded with stuff. Some people feel safe when they keep stashing money away. Hoarding hurts us. When we have more than enough, it is meant to be shared. Give it away.

9) *We long for the good life.*

We suffer from fiscal myopia. Myopia is being near-sighted, seeing only those things which are up close. When we see only that which matters to us, we fail to be far-sighted, looking towards what matters to God and then giving to that cause. We must have a focus beyond living the good life here on earth, and look to our greater life with God in the hereafter.

10) *We practice convenient Christianity.*

Rather than surrender fully to Jesus Christ, we follow Him when we find Him convenient and easy. We pursue the illusion of casual Christianity, instead of following the real Jesus who demands every part of our lives.

In Ted Scofield's Mockingbird blog *"Everybody Else's Problem,"* surveys about greed in America had some surprising results. According to a Zogby poll, people said greed was the most urgent problem in our country. Moreover, a 2014 poll in *Vanity Fair* revealed that seventy-eight percent of Americans disagreed with the widely known Gordon Gekko claim that "Greed is good." Even a poll by *Economist* magazine asked readers, "What is the deadliest sin?" and greed was the top answer. And last, a poll by the BBC showed that although greed is considered one of the seven deadly sins, most people find it to be the least problematic. It is here that we see the problem. Here is the contradiction. We say that greed is the most urgent problem, but we don't admit that greed is *our* problem.[31]

A STORY ABOUT GIVING

Jesus knows that greed grips the human heart. This is why story after story in the Gospels refer to it. Jesus had to confront the reality of our greed. One such story, recounted in the Gospel of Mark, involved a time when Jesus was doing some people watching.

Mark 12:41-44

Jesus sat down opposite the place where the offerings were put and watched the crowd putting their money into the temple treasury. Many rich people threw in large amounts. But a poor widow came and put in two very small copper coins, worth only a few cents. Calling His disciples to him, Jesus said, "Truly I tell you, this poor widow has put more into the treasury than all the others. They all gave out of their wealth; but she, out of her poverty, put in everything—all she had to live on."

People watching. It was a regular pastime for the people who were in Jerusalem for the Feast of Passover. In this final week of His life, we can assume that Jesus was tired, so He sat down. Yet, He wasn't just physically tired—He was tired of what He saw. During each day of the feast, Jews came to the Temple to worship God, and it was then that Jesus did some people watching—and some*thing* about some*one* caught His attention, so much so that He called His disciples to the scene. Jesus wanted to leave His disciples with a serious lesson on life, and we catch some of the intensity of the teaching moment when Jesus began with the words, "Truly, I tell you…" This is a phrase meaning, "Listen up now!" There were three observations that Jesus made while doing His people watching, and He wanted those observations to catch the attention of His disciples.

Expectation

The Jews were doing what was expected of them during Passover, bringing their offerings to God. Let's try and put ourselves there, seeing and hearing what Jesus did. Notice the phrase, "where the offerings were put." Jews put their offerings into shofar chests that were shaped like trumpets. A shofar was the horn of a ram that was blown like a trumpet. This is why these offering receptacles were called trumpets. They were sculpted out of metal, most likely bronze or brass, and they had a wide opening at the top, like the bell of a modern-day trumpet. The trumpet then narrowed and was attached to a chest that contained the coins of the offering. In that day, people did not have currency, but only coins made of gold, silver, and copper.

Imagine what Jesus saw—and heard! Hundreds of thousands of people streamed into Jerusalem for Passover. They jostled one another, standing shoulder-to-shoulder making their way to the offering chests. As they threw in their coins, a clanging sound would ring out as metal hit metal in the wide opening of the trumpet. It was a noisy offering! But Jesus didn't notice the sound. He noticed a widow—and a poor widow at that. The word "poor" that Jesus used here noted that she was in danger of starving. Yet she did something remarkable. The widow put all that she had to live on into the offering box. She threw two small copper coins into the trumpets. The Greek word used for the coins means "thin ones," and our English word leaf is related to this word. So, the poor widow threw in two thin coins, as thin as leaves, which would have made little or no sound at all. She did what God expected of her, and far more. This "more" is what caught the attention of Jesus. In response, He said, "They all gave out of their wealth; but she, out of her poverty, put in everything—all she had to live on."

Motivation

Something else caught the attention of Jesus that day. It was the motivation of the people who gave their offering. Think about how the leaders of the Temple designed the giving system. Why didn't they just build some kind of chest to hold these coins? Why go to all the trouble to sculpt something that looked like the bell of a trumpet? Do you remember Jesus preaching a sermon in the early days of His ministry? Do you remember what He said about the motivation of giving in that sermon? In His Sermon on the Mount, Jesus said, "So when you give to the needy, do not announce it with trumpets, as the hypocrites do in the synagogues and on the streets, to be honored by others. Truly I tell you, they have received their reward in full" (Matthew 6:2). Could it be that there were many people that day throwing in large sums of money, who wanted to be seen, and heard, by others? When wealthy Jews brought their heavy gold coins and threw them into the trumpets, the sound would have been heard in all directions. The echoing clangs would have turned the heads of many people standing nearby. People wanted to be recognized for their generous giving. What motivated the Jews to give their gifts in this manner? Sadly, it had more to do with pride than with humility.

Yet, the motivation of the poor widow was different. Indeed, her two thin coins, which had very little weight and value, would not have been seen or heard by others. But, her offering was seen by Jesus. Her motivation was to honor God, and in her humble generosity, she certainly accomplished that very thing. This story, therefore, shows us the clear difference between wrong motivation and right motivation when it comes to giving.

Devotion

One more thing stands out in this story. Jesus said of the widow that she "put in all that she had to live on," while the others "gave out of their wealth." Here we learn another way to count an offering. Human calculation would say that all the other people gave more based on the enormous amounts they gave to God. Yet, according to heaven's calculation the widow gave more because she kept nothing for herself. Her offering cost her everything. The widow completely trusted in God for her next meal, her next night's sleep, and more. In that ancient culture, a widow was powerless. Women often out lived their husbands, which is why grown children were supposed to care for them. When Jesus said that she put in everything on which she had to live, He reveals that she had no one to help her continue to live. She was alone. She had no Social Security survivor benefits to claim. She had no life insurance policy on her deceased husband to redeem. Moreover, she faced the threat of the Jewish leaders. Just look at what Jesus said about the teachers of the law in the previous verses.

Mark 12:38-40

As He taught, Jesus said, "Watch out for the teachers of the law. They like to walk around in flowing robes and be greeted with respect in the marketplaces, and have the most important seats in the synagogues and the places of honor at banquets. They devour widows' houses and for a show make lengthy prayers. These men will be punished most severely."

Had the teachers of the law already "devoured" this poor widow's house? If so, her two thin coins were the only things of monetary value she had left – and she gave them to God. Her actions shouted devotion, and her devotion to God caught the attention of Jesus that day.

There's an old saying, "Some things never change." Come to think of it, "Some One never changes," and His name is Jesus. "Jesus Christ is the same yesterday, today and forever" (Hebrews 13:8). Jesus doesn't change, and we can assume that He still does some people watching. Could we be the people He is watching, particularly when it comes to our giving? It may be that we struggle with giving because we struggle to accept the three life lessons Jesus gave to His disciples when He taught them about the generous widow. Let's review those lessons, which still apply to us today.

LESSON #1

God measures our giving not by the amount we give to Him, but by the amount we keep for ourselves.

This issue is significant to God because what we do with our money is important to God. Why? What we keep for ourselves matters to Him because it indicates if He really matters to us. What we set aside for God does two things:

1) It limits what we spend on ourselves, and 2) it indicates whether or not God matters most in our lives. Giving to God is not a casual after-thought. Rather, we must give our giving careful forethought. Incredible, significant giving happens when we learn to live with less in the land of more.

LESSON #2

No one is too poor to give.

Jesus wants us to learn this lesson from the poverty-stricken widow. We often think we are too poor to give, but God doesn't buy this excuse. The widow blew that excuse right out of the water. Most of us have been in a life circumstance where we thought we were too poor to give, and so we didn't. No one is too poor to give; not college students, single moms, divorced dads, young married couples, retirees, widows, widowers, the unemployed, the underemployed, those with debt, those starting new jobs. Simply put, no one is too poor to give.

LESSON #3

We will never learn to give to God until we learn to trust God.

I can't speak for you, but as for me, I can't comprehend giving to God "all I have on which to live," as did the poor widow. Her story was not a parable. It actually happened. She gave everything she had on which to live. How would she eat, where would she sleep that night? I want to know. Typically, when we read of this event, we think of it happening once. Yet, peeking around the corner of the verse, I speculate that she was able to put all her money into the offering because she had learned to trust God, and she had found Him more than faithful. This probably wasn't the first time the widow gave all she had, and it would not be the last. She had learned to trust God. Have we? When we die, we trust God for eternal life, so why can't we trust Him for our needs in this life? When we learn to trust God, we will become the kind of people who naturally give to God, and give abundantly.

A Nigerian proverb states: "It's the heart that gives. The fingers just let go." It may be that we struggle with giving because our fingers just won't let go of our money, and the things our money has bought. If we want to conquer our struggle with giving, our heart must change. Only then will we be transformed and start to give generously.

SKIN IN THE GAME

▲ What does Jesus see when He watches you give? Be specific.

▲ Do you struggle with giving to God? If so, why?

▲ Do you use any of the top ten excuses to not give? If so, which one(s)?

▲ Do you know someone who is outrageously generous like the widow? If so, what life lesson do you learn from watching that person give to God?

▲ Of the three life lessons learned from the widow's giving, which one most impacts your thinking? Why?

START GIVING

Los Angeles has a serious water problem. It has nothing to do with drought conditions, but with the condition of their water pipes. The city has a century-old pipe system that fails repeatedly. At times, water mains have fractured, causing massive damage to buildings, homes, and roadways. When a ninety-year old pipe broke beneath Sunset Boulevard recently, more than ten million gallons of water flooded much of the campus of UCLA. City officials are not unaware of the problems. They are slowly—very slowly—replacing the system, and estimates indicate that it will take the equivalent of several lifetimes to install a new, updated water system. Why so long? There is little political motivation. In politics and money, what lies beneath the surface of the ground (literally in this case) is of little importance. Out of sight, out of mind.[32]

What lies beneath the surface is often not a high priority to us. Could that apply to the condition of our hearts, particularly when it comes to giving? We will start giving to God when our hearts transform. After all, it's the heart that gives. The fingers just let go.

Giving to God is an important part of personal financial health because it is an essential part of a healthy relationship with God. We see this truth in a well-known passage about giving. The last book of the Old Testament is Malachi, and it is often overlooked except for one single passage that has to do with giving. But we should not miss the context of this book. The message of Malachi is about much more than giving and contributions. It's about commitment. Malachi gives one example after another of how God's people struggled to stay committed to Him. Of the mere fifty-five verses in the book of Malachi, forty-seven verses are

God speaking to His people about having an authentic, life-long commitment to Him. People in Malachi's day thought of themselves as followers of God, yet the prophet wrote about corrupt priests, unfaithful husbands, and stingy givers. God was looking for evidence that His people were truly committed to Him. But their lives indicated just the opposite. They lacked commitment. James 1:17 states that God doesn't change. This tells us that He is still looking for evidence that we are committed to Him. Giving financially to God is one of the most basic, fundamental, down-to-earth ways of showing Him our commitment. Let's now read the well-known passage.

Malachi 3:8-12

"Will a mere mortal rob God? Yet you rob me. "But you ask, 'How are we robbing you?' "In tithes and offerings. You are under a curse—your whole nation—because you are robbing me. Bring the whole tithe into the storehouse, that there may be food in my house. Test me in this," says the Lord Almighty, "and see if I will not throw open the floodgates of heaven and pour out so much blessing that you will not have room enough to store it. I will prevent pests from devouring your crops, and the vines in your fields will not cast their fruit," says the Lord Almighty. "Then all the nations will call you blessed, for yours will be a delightful land," says the Lord Almighty.

To work through this passage, think of the game show *Truth or Consequences*. This was one of the first television game shows that I watched while growing up, and I remember host Bob Barker closing each episode with the phrase, "…hoping all your consequences are happy ones." This passage from Malachi gives us a lot of truth about giving, and how this truth has consequences. Let's look at the specific truths and consequences from this passage.

Truth: There are types of giving, two in particular—tithes and offerings.

God Himself said we can rob Him "in tithes and offerings." The word "tithe" means tenth, and God commands us to give to Him a tenth of what He enables us to earn. In Malachi 3:6, God states, "I, the Lord, do not change." God *still* expects us to give a tenth of our income to Him because the tithe belongs to God (Leviticus 27:30-32). We rob God when we fail to give Him what is already His. If I put $5 into the offering and call it my tithe, I'm mistaken—unless my income is $50 for that pay period. The word "offering" doesn't mean anything about a ten percent tithe. Therefore, the $5 is not my offering unless I first gave God my tithe. And if we are honest, my $5 gift looks more like a tip given to a waiter than it does a demonstration of my love and gratitude to Him. The Bible doesn't teach token giving.

It is important to note that some people believe that there is no need to tithe because tithing is strictly an Old Testament commandment. Yet, notice what Jesus said in the New Testament.

Matthew 23:23

Woe to you, teachers of the law and Pharisees, you hypocrites! You give a tenth of your spices—mint, dill and cummin. But you have neglected the more important matters of the law—justice, mercy and faithfulness. You should have practiced the latter, without neglecting the former.

Jesus called people to practice justice, mercy, and faithfulness, while continuing to practice tithing. Tithing *is* in the New Testament, and it is affirmed by Jesus, Himself. As we begin growing spiritually, we ask: "How much money do I *have* to give to God?" Then, we grow a little more spiritually mature and ask:

"How much of God's money will I give back to Him?" Yet, we hope to grow into a fully-devoted Christ follower who asks: "How much money do I need to live on so that I can give the rest to God?" That will happen if we bring both our tithes and offerings to God.

Truth: The whole tithe is to be brought to the storehouse. Let's deal with two key words—"whole" and "storehouse." First, we are to bring the whole, entire tithe to God. If you are like me, you had to be taught about the whole tithe. Many people think that the three most difficult words to say are, "I am sorry." But, I think we struggle just as much, if not more, to say three other words: "I don't know." Our pride gets in the way of us admitting that we don't know something. I know it has for me in the past.

Leah is a PK (i.e., preacher's kid). She was raised in the church. When we started dating in college, she was the spiritual giant and I was nothing in comparison. She knew the Word of God. I didn't. She knew Jesus Christ in a personal relationship. I didn't. Leah knew what tithing was—and she tithed. I didn't. So, when we married, Leah taught me how to tithe because I had to admit, "I don't know what tithing is." I didn't know what it was or how it happened.

Giving the whole tithe is not advanced math. We don't need a calculator to calculate a tithe. All we have to do is move a decimal point one space to the left. If our pay check is $550.00, our tithe is $55.00. That's not too difficult. The difficult part comes when the rubber hits the road and it's time to obey God and give the tithe. At the moment we are about to give our tithe, Satan plays with our minds: "Are you sure about this? Think what you can do with that money. You need it for the kids, for the rent, for the car payment, for all kinds of things. You are a fool! Stop this!" Why does Satan strike fear within us when it comes to tithing? Simply put, he fears a person who trusts in and is devoted to God—a person who brings his or her whole tithe and offerings to God as an act of devotion. In short, our giving is a clear indication of our commitment to God. Little giving reflects little commitment.

Now let's consider the storehouse. It was a part of the house of God, and in Malachi's day, the house of God was called the Temple. Though it had been destroyed by the Babylonians years before, it had been rebuilt and sacrifices were again being made at the altar of God (Malachi 1:7-14). Israelites were required to take their tithes to the priests serving at the Temple. The priests were then required to put them into the storehouse (i.e., a place of safekeeping).

Tithes were used to accomplish four key purposes of the Temple: 1) provide for the priests and Levites (i.e., similar to ministers today); 2) provide for the prophets who walked the land declaring the message of God (i.e., similar to missionaries today); 3) provide for widows and orphans (i.e., similar to benevolent help today); and 4) provide for the care and upkeep of the Temple (i.e., similar to maintaining the church building today). When we bring the whole tithe into the local church, it provides for ministers, missionaries, benevolence, and maintenance.

For our entire married life, Leah and I have brought "the whole tithe" to the local church, and we have given offerings in addition to our tithes. We do not view our tithe as generous. Tithing is not an act of generosity. It is an act of obedience. When we tithe, we return to God a portion of what He has already given to us. With our tithes we say to God what King David prayed in 1 Chronicles 29:14:

"Everything comes from you, and we have given you only what comes from your hand." Some people get anxious when they tithe. Why would obeying God make us anxious? If we refuse to tithe, we disobey God and even rob Him of what belongs to Him. Now *that* is what should make us anxious!

Truth: God wants us to put Him to the test. Nowhere else in the Bible does God invite us to test Him, except when it comes to giving Him our tithes and offerings. God said, "Test Me in this…" In Hebrew, "test" means "to try to prove." God challenges us to test Him with our resources. He wants us to actually see His faithfulness at work in our lives. He wants us to learn to trust Him when it comes to our money. He has, He is, and He will prove Himself forever faithful to us when we obey and give our tithes and offerings to Him. Remember, if we trust God to give us the fullness of eternal life when we die, how much more should we trust Him with our tithes while we are alive? If we are not tithing, and yet we trust God to save us from death and the grave, we are being inconsistent.

Consequences: How we respond to the truth about tithing determines the consequences of our being blessed or cursed. God told the people that the entire nation was under a curse because they were robbing Him in tithes and offerings (Malachi 3:9). The word "curse" means to be "hemmed in with obstacles." When we do not bring our tithes and offerings to God, our lives are hemmed in with one obstacle after another. We live from day to day, trying to make ends meet, robbing Peter to pay Paul, and facing repeated challenges. As soon as we work through one problem, another arrives on the scene. When we rob God of tithes and offerings, don't be surprised when we are hemmed in with obstacles. Our actions—or the lack thereof—bring consequences.

In contrast, when we obediently bring the whole tithe to God, He throws open the floodgates and pours out so much blessing that we will not have space to contain it. In Hebrew, the word "blessing" means "favor and benefit." Through a floodgate, which is the spillway of a dam, God pours out His favor and benefits into our lives. What opens the floodgates according to Malachi? Is it prayer? Is it Bible reading? Is it singing loudly in worship? Is it being kind and compassionate to others? No. No. No. No. God said that when we obey by bringing our tithes and offerings to Him, He opens the floodgates, pouring out favor and benefit into our lives. We are blessed by God when we participate in the sacraments of baptism and communion. Likewise, tithing is sacramental in nature because we receive God's favor when we tithe.

The promise of blessing doesn't mean that money will rain down from the sky. Favor and benefit are evidenced in many ways other than monetary gain. Our marriages and families are under His blessing, as well as our work, education, and more. Every aspect of our lives comes under God's favor. God even said, "I will prevent pests from devouring your crops and the vines of your fields will not cast their fruit" (Malachi 3:11). In other words, God works supernaturally to provide for us, and to protect what we have. We call this God's economy. His economy doesn't make sense to us, but it works. When we obey God and bring to Him our tithes and offerings, we put ourselves in the path of His favor and benefits. Actions bring consequences.

Swim against the current. Dare to be different. For many people, the typical "tithe" in America is less than three percent, and only a mere fraction of Christians give that amount to God. Bring the whole tithe and offerings to Him. Don't try tithing. We try a new APP for our phones. We try a new coffee or dessert. When preaching, Jesus said, "So when you give to the needy…" (Matthew 6:2). Jesus did not say, "Try giving to the needy…" He was direct, just like His Father, Who said, "Bring the whole tithe…" Tithing is an act of obedience. In a culture that is addicted to having too much, tithing is an act that will train our hearts to be content to live with less and trust God for His provision.

STRIVE TO GIVE MORE

Research indicates that we tend to overdo it. This does not mean that we over exert ourselves, but rather, we overestimate something about ourselves. Researchers from York University in Canada released a study that shows that both men and women misjudge the intensity of their exercising. Calling this a form of exercise pride, people who exercise have a tendency to overestimate their work-outs.[33]

Could the same be true about our giving? Does pride cause us to over-estimate the amount that we are actually giving to God? This happens easily. We may think that we are generous by tithing on our income and giving additional offerings. But, what if we regularly miss worship services throughout the year and we do not bring our tithes to God for the weeks that we missed? Have we actually tithed, or have we overestimated our giving? Rather than misjudge the amount, let's be sure that we are bringing the whole tithe to God and then strive to give more. Remember, giving more than our tithe is called an offering.

God is pleased with generosity. In 2 Corinthians 8-9, we read of a situation in the early church when believers were challenged to give more than a tithe. The Apostle Paul wrote,

2 Corinthians 9:6-7

"Remember this: whoever sows sparingly will also reap sparingly, whoever sows generously will also reap generously. Each of you should give what he has decided in his heart in his heart to give, not reluctantly or under compulsion, for God loves a cheerful giver."

What this passage does *not* do is to give someone a pass on tithing. Many people say that this passage indicates that the New Testament doesn't teach—or require—tithing. They consider Paul's instruction that "each man should give what he has decided in his heart to give" a license to decide freely the size of the gift, even a gift that is less than a tithe. The problem with this interpretation is that it doesn't consider the context of the passage. Paul wrote to the Christians in the Corinthian church to remind them that they had made a promise to collect a special offering to send to Christians suffering elsewhere (2 Cor. 9:5). Such a generous, special offering had already been collected in Macedonia (2 Cor. 8:1-5), and now Paul was asking the Corinthian Christians to do the same. This offering was above and beyond their tithes. As stated earlier, Jesus affirmed tithing in Matthew 23:23. Ultimately, what Paul was saying was that "each man should give what he has decided in his heart" to give to the *special love offering that was over and above tithes.* This was a call and challenge to the Christians in Corinth to strive to give more.

Notice, too, that this striving to give more impacts God. God loves a cheerful giver (vs. 7), and the word for cheerful in Greek is *hilaros.* Does that look familiar? It should. We derive our English word hilarious from it. Do we give begrudgingly, with a smug look on our faces? Are we reluctant to give, to let go of our money? Knowing that generous giving warms the heart of God, a smile should break across our faces every time we bring to Him our tithes and offerings.

We have a hard time being sacrificial, yet sacrifice is at the heart of generosity. When we willingly go without something so that we can give to others, we become generous. That is what differentiates giving from generosity. Generous giving begins when we say no to ourselves and yes to others. We experience inconvenience. When we give generously of our time, we are saying no to our busy schedules and yes to others. Our schedules have been inconvenienced. When we give generously of our talents and skills, we are saying no to our own pursuits and yes to sharing with others. We inconvenience our pursuits. When we give generously of our money and resources, we are saying no to our own desires and yes to the needs of others. We are inconvenienced on what we want to spend on ourselves.

Let's be painfully honest at this point. Saying no to ourselves will be inconvenient at times, but that is the nature of sacrifice. C.S. Lewis said it well, "I do not believe one can settle how much we ought to give. I am afraid the only safe rule is to give more than we can spare. In other words, if our expenditures on comforts, luxuries, amusements, etc., is up to the standard common among those with the same income as our own, we are probably giving away too little. If our charities do not at all pinch or hamper us, I should say they are too small. There ought to be things we should like to do and cannot do because our charities expenditure excludes them."[34]

I was born and raised along Lake Michigan, and I've made many trips to Chicago. It is a city that has a unique history. In October 1871, the Great Chicago Fire destroyed much of the city, burning one building after another. Surprisingly, the Chicago River even caught fire! In those years, the Chicago River was a slow moving sewer for the city, and the famous Union Stock Yards dumped all of their animal waste directly into the river. The massive waste in the water was highly combustible. Not only did Chicago struggle to survive in the aftermath of the fire, but thousands of people were dying of waterborne illnesses, such as cholera and typhoid fever caused by waste flowing into Lake Michigan from the river. City leaders, therefore, decided to undertake one of the most daring engineering projects yet attempted in human history. They would try to reverse the flow of the Chicago River. Doing so would purify their drinking water coming from Lake Michigan. After digging twenty-eight miles of canals and setting many locks and gates, the project was finally completed on January 2, 1900. On that day, a sluice was opened and a wall of water rushed into the canal system and flowed with such force into the Chicago River that it reversed the flow of the river. Chicago grew and flourished from that day forward, becoming the third largest city in America.[35]

What if we were to reverse the flow in our lives? Rather than keep taking from God, what if we started to generously give back to God what we receive from Him? More than a city can flourish. Our individual lives will flourish because our obedience in giving results in living under God's favor and blessing. Is it time to reverse the flow?

SKIN IN THE GAME

▲ Winston Churchill said, "We make a living by what we get, but we make a life by what we give." What kind of a life are you making by your giving? Be specific.

▲ Should we tithe on our net or gross income? Why?

▲ Have you put God to the test by tithing? If not, why not? If so, how did He open the floodgates of heaven and pour out blessings on you? (Remember, think beyond monetary blessings.)

▲ Have you said no to yourself so you could say yes to someone else? If so, how did you feel when you gave generously in that moment?

Chapter 11
The *Real* Profit

"What good is it for someone to gain the
whole world, yet forfeit their soul?"
Mark 8:36

Though I excelled in school, math was and is not my strength. The world of mathematics suddenly changed for me when letters of the alphabet appeared alongside numbers. I can crunch numbers well, read profit and loss statements, calculate ratios from statements of financial position, but don't ask me to try and solve a problem from your calculus class. I struggle with those equations.

Do you struggle when it comes to the equation in this book? If we want to restore financial health to our lives, we must learn to live with less in the land of more. If we want to be free of the bondage of debt, we must admit that we owe too much because we have purchased too much. The equation is not difficult to understand. It is just difficult to pursue. That is why we must be intentional.

PRINCIPLES + PRACTICES = REAL PROFIT

When we embrace four specific biblical principles, and then add to those principles four specific practices, it will result in *real* profit. When we authentically embrace the principles of gratitude, contentment, trust (in God), and humility, we begin a journey toward financial health. And when we add to those principles the consistent practices of debt-free living, saving, budgeting, and generous giving, the journey becomes all the more exciting and transforming. The *real* profit has more to do with the quality of our lives than with the worldly measurements of success, like dollars in the bank, size of investment portfolios, square footage under roof, number of acres owned, and more.

When our financial house is in order, we experience *real* profits. Our marriages become healthier and the shouting matches about money soon disappear. Our families grow healthier because there is less stress about burdensome debt. Our homes become happier places because what really matters in life becomes a priority. Financial health enables people to sleep well at night, instead of tossing and turning on their beds—particularly on a $2,000 mattress which they financed for forty-eight months at 18 percent interest. Some equations are quite difficult, but the formula for financial health and wellbeing is one that each of us can, and must, pursue if we want to be free.

THE END RESULT

One of my hobbies is running. Over the years, I've completed some distance events, and what I have learned is that the only way I can complete a marathon is one step at a time. To finish a marathon, I must fight the urge to focus on where I am in the moment, and intentionally focus on the finish line. This is why when I have run marathons with friends, the finish line has been the focus of our conversation during the race. Though we ran past mile markers, we kept talking about mile marker 26.2—the finish line. The same goes for us. We must stay focused on the end.

In much the same way, Jesus talked about the finish line of life, and He did so on many occasions. He asked people a penetrating question: "What good is it for someone to gain the whole world, yet forfeit their soul?" (Mark 8:36) Jesus preached about the road being narrow and the gate being small that leads into eternal life. Few people find it (Matthew 7:14). Could it be that the majority of people do not finish well because they do not focus on the spiritual goal of eternal life? Instead, do they have a greater focus on financially enjoying the present moment? What good is it if we gain the whole world financially and die spiritual paupers?

Forbes publishes an annual list of the world's billionaires, and when we compare the lists from year to year, we discover that we are living in an era of unprecedented wealth. The ranks of the wealthy continue to grow along with their individual holdings. When Forbes announced the list of billionaires for 2015, a record 1,826 people made the list. Not only is the number of billionaires staggering, but so also, are their stockpiles of money and the things that money can buy.[36] Having such wealth is not sinful, but what happens when we achieve financial success, and we haven't surrendered our lives to Jesus Christ? At the moment we die, we discover that we are spiritually bankrupt. We have gained the whole world, yet we have done so at cost of our souls.

As mentioned earlier, former billionaire Bernie Madoff "made off" with billions of dollars of money that did not belong to him. Madoff led the largest Ponzi scheme in the history of our nation. Pleading guilty to multiple fraud-related felonies, Madoff was sentenced to 150 years in prison. His new "mansion" is a medium security prison cell measuring eight by ten feet, and he shares it with a roommate. He lost everything. Though he once handled literally billions of dollars, he is now not allowed to have even a handful of quarters in the prison. Worse yet, he lost his family and friends. Madoff said that while "I miss everything," the estrangement from his family has been hardest to bear, adding that "I don't have anything to live for."[37] He and his wife are now estranged from one another. His youngest son has no intention of forgiving his father or speaking to him. His eldest son committed suicide. Though Madoff gained the whole world with record profits (though illegal), he ultimately lost his wealth, his freedom, and his family. What good is it if we gain the whole world?

Our names do not appear on *Forbes'* list of billionaires, yet we are financially rich in comparison to the remainder of the world. We are as much at risk of forfeiting our souls as the next person. *Real* profits in life focus on quality relationships with family and friends—and most importantly—with Jesus Christ. Don't pursue the fake profits of this world, which focus on quantities of money and the things that money can buy. What would it profit or benefit us to gain everything we want in this life—material goods, education, a reputation, accomplishments, and more—if we don't have Christ? Without Jesus, we have—and are—quite literally nothing.

Life is a marathon, not a sprint. We must keep the end in view. Look past the present moment. In Luke 12:16-21, Jesus told the story of the man who had many barns, but he wanted still bigger barns in which to store all of his grain and goods. The zinger of that story was when Jesus brought it to an end. The parable did not have a typical fairy-tale ending of living happily ever after. To the contrary, God tells the guy that his life would be required of him. The barn guy would die on that very night. The parable ends with a solemn and pointed question: "Then who will get what you have prepared for yourself?" (vs. 20). The parable applies to us just as much as it did for the barn guy. This is why Jesus said to the crowd listening to Him, "This is how it will be with whoever stores up things for themselves but is not rich toward God" (vs. 21). If we gain the whole world but God means nothing to us, we have nothing to look forward to in eternity but loss.

One of my favorite box games is Monopoly. When I play it, watch out. I intend to win. There have been times in the Johnson household when the game has gone on for hours as I financially conquered one opponent after another. I pile cash in front of me, hold the deeds to all of the properties and develop them with hotels. Then, reality usually sets in because Leah has dinner on the table. What? I think, "You've got to be kidding me!" Sure thing, the game is over and it goes back into the box and is put on the shelf for another day. Come to think of it, we are going to be put into a box someday. Like the barn guy, our lives will be required of us. We will die. Death can't be escaped (unless Jesus returns sooner). No one receives a "get out of dying free card." We will die and go into a box. We will take nothing with us. The proverbial U-Haul truck won't go with us to the cemetery. We came into this world with nothing, and we will exit this life with nothing. Life is not a game. Your eternity and mine is real. Do not gain the whole world and forfeit your soul. We must surrender our lives to Christ.

WHERE IS OUR FOCUS?

Matthew 6:22-23

The eye is the lamp of the body. If your eyes are healthy, your whole body will be full of light. But if your eyes are unhealthy, your whole body will be full of darkness. If then the light within you is darkness, how great is that darkness!

When Jesus used this metaphor, He wasn't referring to a person's actual eyes and the amount of light the eyes permit into the body. His metaphor referred to a person's perspective in life. In other words, what captures his or her attention? What is his or her focus? Good eyes refer to a person who has a heart that is ready to give greatly and to share generously with others. In contrast, bad eyes refer to a person whose focus is on self.

What about our focus? Are we focused on God and what matters to Him, or on ourselves? If our perspective in life is good, we won't be looking at the latest, greatest piece of gadgetry, and we won't be focused on money and the things that money can buy. If our perspective in life is good, we will be focused on what matters to God. But if our perspective is bad, we will be drawn to things that intrigue and potentially entrap us. Is it any wonder that commercials and advertisements so easily entice us? Marketing experts are trained to make stuff appeal to us and get us to think that we can't live another day without whatever it is they are selling. When our eyes are bad, our financial health is poor because we overextend ourselves financially.

Most people have had an eye examination at some point in their life. Many are diagnosed with myopia, meaning they are near-sighted (i.e., seeing that which is close up). We can also struggle with a form of *spiritual* myopia, a common condition when we focus on what is up close to us. Spiritual myopia happens when we focus too easily on what matters to us. Perhaps we need a spiritual eye exam. After all, Christians must regularly examine their lives. Think about this. When we take communion, we examine ourselves. The Apostle Paul told the Christians in Corinth to "examine yourselves to see whether you are in the faith…" (2 Corinthians 13:5). He also wrote that "everyone ought to examine themselves before they eat of the bread and drink from the cup" (1 Corinthians 11:28). As followers of God and stewards of His kingdom, we should regularly examine how well we are living for God.

When God is our focus, we will move in His direction. Like a pilot who makes continual course corrections because of strong head winds, we need to make continual course corrections because of the strong pull of our culture. The pattern of the world is always away from God. We must therefore consider whether we are swimming against or with the current of the culture. We must never forget that we are called to be strong salt and bright light in this world. The culture should never change us; rather, we should change the culture. So, where is our focus? What matters to us? If we're pursuing money and the things that money can buy, our eyes will be bad. If our focus is on what matters to God, our eyes will be good.

WHO DO WE SERVE?

Matthew 6:24

No one can serve two masters. Either you will hate the one and love the other or you will be devoted to one and despise the other. You cannot serve both God and money.

The word "serve" means to work as a slave. A slave is the property of a single master. In the first century, two masters rarely shared slaves, but when they did, it led to conflict and divided interests. In this verse, Jesus taught that there had to be absolute loyalty to one master. In light of that truth, He was teaching that a person could not be a slave to both God and money. This statement certainly came true for Judas Iscariot. He had to choose between money and Jesus. In the end, Judas chose thirty pieces of silver instead of his Savior, Jesus Christ.

Do we want money more than a Savior? Are we serving Almighty God or the American dollar? Money bosses us around when God should be our Master. And let's be honest, money is powerful. It's like a strong drink 150 proof. Taken straight or mixed with many lovely things, money is an intoxicating substance to us. When we hold our stuff with a tight grip, it's a sign that our stuff holds on to us. When this happens, we are no longer holding on to God. Either God is our Master or He isn't. If we are dividing our loyalty between God and money, we've already lost. *Real* profit results when we surrender our lives to Christ, making God our one and only Master.

We must remember that we are not owners, but stewards. God owns it all and He has entrusted it to our care. One of my favorite verses is Psalm 24:1. It reads, "The earth is the Lord's and everything in it; the world, and all who live in it." All things belong to Him. Even our own lives belong to Him, if surrendered to Him. This is why Paul says, "...Jesus Christ, who gave Himself for us to redeem us from all wickedness and to purify for Himself a people that are His very own, eager to do what is good" (Titus 2:13-14). God redeemed us. We belong to Him, and as His sons and daughters, we live as stewards, not as owners. We are redeemed people.

We don't use the word "redemption" very often today, but it is a great word. It reminds me of my childhood. Do any of us remember growing up when our moms collected S&H green stamps? After paying for her groceries, the cashier handed my mom dozens of S&H green stamps, and it was my job to lick 'em and stick 'em in stamp books. Once we filled a number of stamp books with hundreds—if not thousands—of stamps, we took them to the S&H Green Stamp "redemption center" to trade them for something we wanted. I wanted a motorized model race car. Mom wanted TV trays. God did something similar with us. He redeemed us by trading in His one and only Son, because God wanted us! God *bought* us back after we became lost to sin. This is why we are not our own.

The Apostle Paul wrote: "Do you not know that your bodies are temples of the Holy Spirit, who is in you, whom you have received from God? You are not your own; you were bought at a price. Therefore honor God with your bodies" (1 Corinthians 6:19-20). This should prompt us to live differently than the world. Let us become the kind of people that can pray like this each and every day: "God, what do You want me to do with this, Your body? Thanks for the gift of a new day. How do you want me to spend Your day…Your money? Where do you want me to study, to work? What do You want me to do with this, Your life?"

What if every Christian—the world over—lived and prayed this way? What if every one of us made our time, our talents, our treasures fully available to God? What if every one of us cared for our bodies as the holy temples that they actually are? Just think what would happen, how our individual lives and the lives of people around us would change, if our minds were entirely committed to God? What if we lived surrendered lives to Christ each day? Our finances would be healthy. Our marriages and families would be whole. The world would be a different place.

FINISH WELL

William Borden grew up in Chicago and graduated from high school in 1904. His family owned Borden Dairy, which was a multi-million-dollar company at the turn of the twentieth century. For his high school graduation present, his parents gave him a trip around the world. William was impacted by the sights that he saw and by the people he met. The rest of the world was so different from his world in Chicago. Young Borden returned home carrying the weight of the world on his shoulders for those who suffered around the world. He decided to pursue a career in world missions, and he wrote in the back of his Bible two simple words: "No reserves."

William Borden attended Yale University, and he held nothing back in reserve. He started a prayer group that grew to hundreds, and it transformed life on campus. By his senior year, one thousand of Yale's thirteen hundred students were meeting in small groups across campus. Borden also led a student ministry so that every student on campus would hear the Gospel of Jesus Christ. His passion for hurting people grew more intense. He often worked with the outcasts and homeless who lived near the campus. When he graduated from Yale, William Borden never wavered from his decision to pursue world missions, and again, he wrote two simple words in the back of his Bible: "No retreats."

In his early adult years, he was offered many lucrative positions in the family business, but declined all of them. After graduation, he immediately went to Egypt to learn Arabic. He accepted a missionary position to work with Muslims through China Inland Mission. While doing language study in Egypt, he contracted spinal meningitis, and within a month, twenty-five-year-old William

Borden was dead. Just before he died, he wrote two more simple words in his Bible: "No regrets."[38]

No reserves. No retreats. No regrets. We can say the same if we surrender our lives to Jesus Christ. We will then receive the *real* profit – eternal life in the hereafter. There is no greater return than what we receive when we surrender our lives to Jesus Christ. While we focus on the finish line of this marathon we call life, let's learn to live with less in the land of more. We'll be glad we did.

SKIN IN THE GAME

▲ How do you define real profit? Describe it. Be specific.

▲ Knowing that life comes to an end for all of us, what kind of a legacy do you hope to leave behind—and for whom?

▲ Are you serving—even slaving for—two masters (God and money)?

▲ Have you surrendered your life to Jesus Christ? If not, why not?

▲ What changes would you need to make to be able to say like William Borden, "No regrets?"

Endnotes

[1] "New Crisis is Bringing Old Lessons into Focus," *Indianapolis Star* (10/13/08).

[2] "Greece's Debt Crisis Explained," *The New York Times* (7/27/15).

[3] "Puerto Rico defaults on $72B debt," *USA Today* (8/4/15).

[4] "Failure is Your Friend" *Freakonomics* Radio Podcast/full transcript (6/4/14)

[5] http://www.wvcuiture.org/history/wvhs1504.html

[6] *Spider-Man*, Columbia Pictures, 2002.

[7] Derek Thompson, "The 100-Year March of Technology in 1 Graph," *The Atlantic* (4-7-12).

[8] Robert Laura, "Pastor Rick Warren Is Well Prepared for A Purpose Driven Retirement," *Forbes.com*; 3/21/13.

[9] David Hockman, "Don't Let the Burger Fool You," *AARP* (October-November, 2012).

[10] Mark Batterson, *The Grave Robber* (Grand Rapids, MI: Baker Books; 2014), p. 191.

[11] http://news.bbc.co.uk/2/hi/uk_news/1535936.stm

[12] Haugen & Boutros, *The Locust Effect* (Oxford, England: Oxford University Press, 2014), p. 101.

[13] Dallas Willard, *The Divine Conspiracy: Rediscovering Our Hidden Life in God* (San Francisco, CA: Harper, 1997), p. 25.

[14] Christian Rudder, *Dataclysm: Who We Are When We Think No One's Looking* (Crown, 2014), pp. 63-64.

[15] Nik Wallenda with David Ritz, *Balance: A Story of Faith, Family and Life on the Line* (New York, New York: Faith Words, 2013), p. 20.

[16] David A. Seamands, *Healing for Damaged Emotions* (Victor Books, 1981), p. 23.

[17] Karen Cheney, "Don't Let Debt Weight You Down," *Money*, May 2012, p. 29.

[18] https://en.wikipedia.org/wiki/I_Want_It_All_(Queen_song)

[19] http://www.bpnews.net/16264

[20] Kregg Hood, *Escape the Debt Trap* (Fort Worth, TX: Prime Source Providers, 2003), p. 7.

[21] http://www.cbsnews.com/news/earning-75000-and-living-paycheck-to-pay-check/

[22] Tim Suttle, *Shrink* (Grand Rapids, MI: Zondervan, 2014), pp. 107-08.

[23] USA Snapshots, *Indianapolis Star*, 8/3/15.

[24] Ian Deitch, "Israeli woman mistakenly junks $1 million mattress," www.ap.org (Associated Press), 6/10/09.

[25] http://www.philanthropyroundtable.org/almanac/hall_of_fame/oseola_mccarty

[26] Peter Dunn, "Hate it or not, you have to have a budget," *Indianapolis Star*, 7/19/15.

[27] Mihret Yohannes, "German rallying cry is 'cash only,'" *Indianapolis Star*, 7/18/15.

[28] Danny Vink, "The FDA's Food Calorie Labels Probably Won't Make People Healthier," *The Science of Us*, 11/26/14.

[29] Chris Taylor, *"The Last Taboo; Why Nobody Talks About Money"* Reuters (3/27/14).

[30] John Dickerson, *The Great Evangelical Recession* (Grand Rapids, MI: Baker Books, 2013), pp. 178-79.

[31] Ted Scofield "Everybody Else's Problem, Part 2," *Mockingbird blog* (7/28/15).

[32] http://www.latimes.com/local/cityhall/la-me-pipe-rupture-20140807-story.html

[33] Melissa Dahl "Your Workout isn't as Intense as You Think," *Science of Us* (6/17/14).

[34] C.S. Lewis, *Mere Christianity* (New York, New York: Touchstone, 1996), p. 82.

[35] http://articles.chicagotribune.com/2012-01-01/site/ct-per-flash-riverreversal-0101-20120102_1_chicago-river-polluted-river-lake-michigan-water

[36] http://www.nbcnews.com/business/economy/record-number-billionaires-2015-including-mj-forbes-says-n315486

[37] http://www.politico.com/story/2014/03/bernie-madoff-interview-104838

[38] http://involve.christian-union.org/site/News2?page=NewsArticle&id=7569

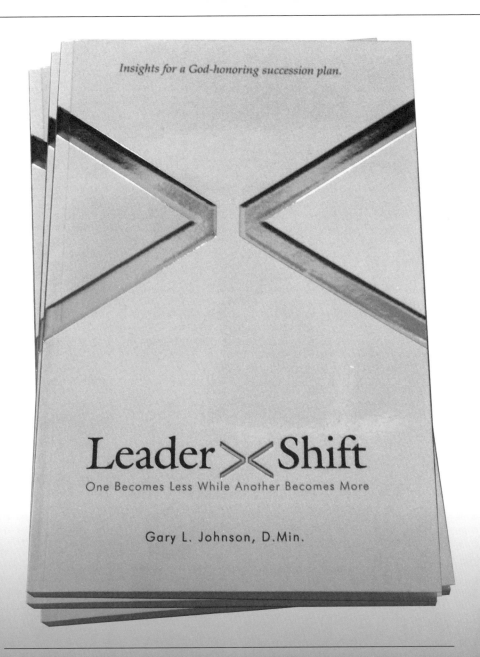

Leader><Shift addresses the complex challenge of succession planning for the local church or para-church ministry, and provides both a logical and biblical strategy for a God-honoring succession plan.

Multiple copies can be purchased for every person on your leadership team by writing to gary@e2elders.org.

TOO
MUCH
LIVING WITH LESS
IN THE LAND OF MORE

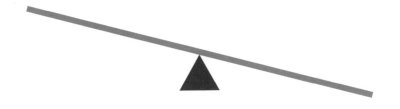

Multiple copies can
be purchased at
discount by writing to
gary@e2elders.org.